Happily Godless
A Young Adult's Guide to Atheism

D1446473

Paul Donovan

PublishAmerica
Baltimore

First printing

ISBN: 1-4241-9963-8
PUBLISHED BY PUBLISHAMERICA, LLLP
www.publishamerica.com
Baltimore

Printed in the United States of America

For Tim

A brave thinker,

A true friend.

Acknowledgements

I would like to thank my "real-life" friends whose conversations over the years helped to form this book: Ben, Brandon, Jason, Joey, Nick, Drew, Michael-Lee, Dottie, and Rob.

I would also like to thank my "xanga gang" for their countless blog posts and comments that helped shape the book and give me inspiration and encouragement: atheistthoughts, NikBv, HotNachoCheese, NQbass7, An_Atheist_View, JB_Fidei_Defensor, godgone, zebra_slut, master_stghm, Skepticism_Is_A_Good_Thing, bittersunday, TheTroubador, Retrovertigo, ariella_1, HassSaugt, hecticmuse, Agnostics_R_Us, crackcannon, GodAintGood and jonny_quest.

And finally, I'd like to thank my family, even though they don't believe most of what I wrote in this book.

Introduction:
Don't Tell the Teenagers!

While I was writing this book, I told a friend about it. He is a high school teacher, like myself, and has constant contact with young people. I told him that I was writing a book, for high school and college aged people, that dealt with an honest look at how critical thinking and logic show that many beliefs of Christianity can't be true. My friend got uncomfortable right away.

"Now, Paul," he said, looking a little worried, "I know I've got my own problems with religion. But I don't think it's a good idea to bring all this up to kids."

"Why not?" I asked. "What are we trying to hide? And you know how important it is for people to learn critical thinking skills."

"Yeah, but I'm glad that I was raised as a Christian. It gave me a good moral belief system. It's good to have some values like that."

"I get it," I said. "My book isn't going to tell people to be immoral. Showing problems with the existence of God and the truth of Christianity is not the same thing as telling them to be immoral."

"But," he replied, still not buying it, "how else are you going to give kids the basics of being good people?"

"Not by convincing them that fairy tales are true. If you need to believe in supernatural events to convince yourself that treating people nice is how you should behave, then you have issues."

I could see that I was still having trouble convincing him.

That's one of the biggest fears that I've come across when bringing up the idea of atheist or agnostic teenagers. While many adults privately admit that they don't believe everything the largest religion in America says, they try very hard to not share those doubts with teenagers and young adults (or anyone else, for that matter). They are worried that if young people decided to not believe in God and Jesus, then we'll have kids who do drugs and have sex! Or worse!

Of course, a lot of young people today don't base their behaviors regarding sex or alcohol or drugs on their belief in God. I know Christian teens who have sex and do drugs. I know non-religious teens that don't. Besides that, the idea that kids must be protected from the truth is insulting. Young adults today are able to handle the truth. They're not fragile, innocent flowers that will wilt under the sun of reality. They can be smart and mature enough to figure out their own place in the world without relying on fantasy. In fact, I think that continually lying to kids until they're suddenly 18 and living on their own just makes things worse in the long run.

Like many other people, I think it's terrible for parents to just label their kids are the same religion as they are. Can a 5-year-old kid really be Catholic? Or Lutheran? Or anything else? They're happy when they can tie their own shoes. How are they going to decide the truths of the universe? But parents automatically assume that kids have the same religious beliefs as they do. And society just goes along with it. Even as kids get older, most parents try to make sure their kids don't get any funny ideas about being something else.

As kids grow up, parents like to teach them that if you want to buy something, you need to shop around, compare prices and features, and pick the best deal. But when it comes to figuring out your religious beliefs and deciding the base of your ethical system, most people don't want kids doing that. Don't shop around, because Christianity is automatically the best deal.

But what are people afraid of? If Christianity really is the "best deal," then shopping around will only prove it. Christianity gets treated with a strange double standard in society today. The fact that you are not encouraged to question Christianity seems a little suspicious, doesn't it?

As someone that has worked extensively with young adults, I know that issues of religion, morality, and meaning are on their minds a lot. But they don't know where to go for answers when their inherited religious tradition doesn't seem to help. Sometimes they don't even know what questions to ask. They are confused and often feel like they are the only ones confused because everyone else seems so confident about what they believe. Maybe you are one of those confused people. If so, my heart hurts for you.

And that's what this book is about. It's insulting and disrespectful for society to try to keep you from questioning the very base of reality. It's OK to ask questions, and look for answers. If you feel something isn't quite right, it probably isn't. This book may give you some answers you wanted to know. It may tell you things that you didn't know you wanted to know. It may open up new questions. That's healthy.

Question everything. That's your job as young adults.

Part Zero

Interesting Stuff
You Need to Know First

Why You Might Be Reading This

There are a few different kinds of people who might be reading this book:

First, there are young atheists who will see this book and say, "Finally! A book written for me! I'm not the only kid around who feels this way!" And you might be thinking about sharing this book with your family or friends.

Or maybe you don't consider yourself an actual atheist, but you have serious questions about what you believe. Questions that you can't seem to get straight answers to. Maybe you don't even know exactly who to ask. Or what to ask.

Maybe you are a young Christian who is offended by the very idea of a book like this, because it might end up leading young people straight to Hell. If this is you, I would encourage you to read this book with an open mind.

Or maybe you're a parent or teacher who found this book and are curious as to what kind of message is given out to young people about this controversial topic. Maybe you are alarmed at this book; maybe you are glad. Hopefully you won't censor what young adults read. They are old enough to start making some real decisions for themselves.

To all of you, I say welcome. I would welcome your reactions to this book.

Why I Wrote This Book

As a math teacher, I know that the ability to think critically is absolutely necessary. Thinking critically means that you don't believe something just because somebody tells you to. One of the main jobs of teenagers is to question authority and start to figure things out for themselves. I think that is one of the best things about being a teenager, and one of the healthiest. Thinking for yourself is the best thing you can do.

America is a pretty religious country. And while there are many religions in America, the most influential is Christianity. And even though it affects many parts of people's lives, nobody is really encouraged to question it. Christian children learn what the world is about from their parents, who learned it from their parents. And so on and so on. Going to church just cements it in.

Yet most Christians remain totally ignorant about their own religion. People aren't encouraged to read the Bible and think about it. That's because if they did, churches would be in trouble.

The fact is, a lot of scholars have looked at the Bible. And they have come to conclusions that will shock and offend many conservative Christians. But just because some people will be offended doesn't mean it's not true. And it certainly doesn't mean we shouldn't talk about it.

So this book will talk about it. The things that we will look at in these pages are not new, even though they may sound kind of shocking. But just because these ideas aren't new doesn't mean they're well known. You see, Bible historians and scholars mostly write for other historians and scholars. This does include some religious leaders, who no doubt know these things. But the general public doesn't often get to see this stuff. Partly because most religious authorities don't really want their church members to read it. But also partly because most of it is not written for regular people. That is starting to change, but only very slowly. I hope this book is a small part of that change.

And after all the research I've done, I haven't found one single book that was written for teens and young adults. I don't know why that is; perhaps because people are afraid to give young people access to this. Perhaps because scholars think young people aren't smart enough to understand it all. I'm not sure.

But one thing I am sure of is that this information is important. It's important for individuals, and it's important for America. And it's especially important for young people, who need all the information they can find as they start to make sense of the world around them.

What Is a Skeptic?

When people use the word *skeptic*, they sometimes mean it as someone who is kind of grumpy, kind of a jerk, who always ruins everybody's fun by saying they don't believe it. But this is a stereotype often applied to skeptics by people who, well, don't like skeptics, who don't like to have their own ideas challenged. A skeptic is really just someone who uses reason to figure things out, and who doesn't automatically believe something just because someone says it's true. When a skeptic hears an interesting or unusual claim, the typical response is "That sounds great! Now, how do you know this?" If you can't back up your claim, it would be kind of foolish to believe it. Interestingly, it is easy to be a skeptic when it comes to things we don't already believe. It's much harder to be a skeptic about your own beliefs.

Beliefs can—and do—enter into our lives and minds without us being really aware of it. We get beliefs from watching things, touching things, and listening to things. We most often listen to people like parents and teachers, who we trust to give us true and valuable things to believe.

But what about ideas like Santa Claus? A lot of children grow up believing in Santa Claus. Children are told to believe in Santa by their own parents. And there are books that talk about Santa Claus. Very old books! Surely they wouldn't lie! Presents appear under the Christmas tree overnight. When I was a kid, I left cookies and milk for Santa before I went to bed and when I woke up, they were all eaten! All these things prove that Santa is real!

Right?

Eventually the child learns that there is no such person as Santa. She might develop suspicions when she learns that she has to be asleep before he shows up. She might wonder how he can appear at so many stores at the same time. If she can read history books, she might wonder why they never mention someone as extraordinary as Santa Claus. She might realize that all the physical evidence, from presents to cookies, can be done by regular people. You don't need Santa to explain them. Eventually, one Christmas Eve, she may hear Santa in the living room, and she may sneak down to meet him, but instead of meeting a jolly old fat man, she will see her parents. Or perhaps she won't figure it out, so her parents have to eventually tell her the truth before she gets made fun of at school for believing in something that doesn't really exist.

It takes awhile for us to develop skepticism. It's hard for us to accept that things we are told, even by caretakers, aren't always true. That we can be fooled by things because we didn't think critically about all the evidence. I believed that Santa ate my cookies because I didn't think about the possibility that it was just my dad that ate them. Once I believed in Santa, I found all kinds of things to justify it. One Christmas Eve I looked out the window and saw a blinking red light on a passing airplane. Immediately I thought it was Rudolph. It wasn't until I was in kindergarten, when a classmate told me that Santa didn't exist, and my parents didn't argue, that I realized I had been fooled.

You probably already see where I am going with this. Religion can be approached by the same methods. We are told by our parents (and then by our religious leaders) that Jesus is the savior of the world. We see books written about him. We hear about miracles. We figure that the people that care about us, the books that help people, would never lie to us. Why would they lie to us about such important things?

That's a great question.

While this book will not try to answer that question, the fact of the matter is, the case for the reality of the Bible's claims of Jesus is no stronger than that of Santa Claus.

People who are skeptics about the claims of Christianity and other religions will often be led to either atheism or agnosticism. While the technical definitions of each one of those words is still argued about, people generally agree on the basics. A **theist** is someone that believes in God. Theists then divide themselves up according to a specific religion. An **atheist** is someone that doesn't believe in God. An **agnostic** is someone that thinks that the question of God's existence can't be answered one way or another.

What This Book Is

This book is a skeptical look at religion. It is an introduction to atheist viewpoints and beliefs, and why, despite such a religious culture, a lot of people aren't religious. It is an open door for young people to explore their questions and doubts. Hopefully, it will enable them to feel like less of a freak for questioning religion. It is a way to give young non-believers comfort and fellowship.

This book is also a call for religious people to understand why people are atheists. It is designed to show young Christians that atheists are not lost, misguided, or just looking for excuses to do bad things. It will (hopefully) encourage young Christians to stop trying to convert atheists, and to stop discriminating against atheists when they don't convert to Christianity.

Specifically, this is a book that examines the problems with the basic beliefs of Christianity, including the very existence of God and the holiness of Jesus. It will look at the false claims that America was founded as a Christian country. Finally, it will look at the myths that some people believe about atheism.

Some readers will automatically feel offended and ask why I'm picking on Christianity. After all, questions about the existence of God apply to many more people than just Christians. Why do I focus on them?

Yes, there are many different religions in the world, and many different societies influenced by different religions. However, in the country in which I live and work, that religion is Christianity. A belief system like Christianity, that carries so much power and influence, should be open to examination to see if it deserves as much power as it has. As you will see, logic and history leads many people to believe that the answer is "no."

The main point I want to get across to Christians who read this is that they should recognize that their beliefs are based on faith, not logic or reason. Logic and reason are important in Christianity, but only *after* you have the faith that it's already true. Atheists can't even make the first step that Christians do. Faith does not rely on scientific evidence, which atheists ask for.

What This Book Is Not

One of the things that is very important for you to understand is that this book is not the one and only authority on skepticism and atheism. I don't want this to become a "Bible" for young atheists. That would be very hypocritical of me. I did not make this stuff up all by myself, and to pretend I did would also be plagiarism. No, this book is based on research from many different books and sources. What I did is try to pull all the interesting stuff together here so that young people can still get all this without being intimidated by books that are a lot harder to read.

This book is also not meant to be a textbook. I don't want this book to feel like homework. I wanted to keep the book interesting, using the same logic and critical thinking skills that people should use in all other aspects of their lives. Don't' forget that this book is simply an introduction. The topics we'll talk about here have whole books written about them by scholars who devote their lives to studying this. What I want to do is show you where to start, to show young people that they have all the abilities and skills they need to make their own decisions about religion, based on logic and historical fact.

This means, then, that there will probably be ideas presented here that you will want to study more on your own. Unlike most religious leaders, I completely encourage you to do so. In fact, I would be disappointed if you read this book and then just considered yourself to know all you need to. I have included references and bibliographical information for every source I've used to write this book, and even a few that I haven't. I hope you find some that seem interesting and look into them yourself.

This book is not about just bashing Christians. I know many nice people who are strong Christians. This book is not an angry tirade about how all religion should be wiped off the face of the earth. This book is not trying to convert everybody to atheism.

However, while not going out of my way to insult Christians, this book is not a defense of Christianity. This book will explain what some problems with Christianity are. How you take this information is up to you. Some people will undoubtedly be offended at this book. That's just the way people are.

A Note on the Bible

One book you might really want to have with you as you read this one is the Bible. The best way to see what the Bible really says is to read it yourself. Now, you don't *have* to have your own Bible with you to enjoy this book, but if you do, it will be easy to see for yourself what I'm talking about.

Let me give a brief explanation of what the Bible is, for those people who aren't exactly sure.

The Bible isn't actually one book. It's a whole lot of smaller books written at different times and different places that were collected together. The Bible is divided into two sections, the Old Testament (sometimes abbreviated OT) and the New Testament (abbreviated as, logically, NT). The OT starts with the creation of the Earth and goes all the way up to the birth of Jesus.

The OT is basically written about and for Jews, because it contains their holy books and is full of stories about the beginning of the Jewish people and the rules that God wanted them to follow. The New Testament is the story of Jesus and his life and the beginning of Christianity. Since Jesus was a Jew (Christianity wasn't started until way after Jesus died), Christians keep the Old Testament around as valuable scripture, but not as valuable as the New Testament. Jews don't believe that Jesus was the Son of God, or the Savior, and don't think he was anything but a good teacher, so they don't accept the New Testament as a holy book (this has caused much trouble for the Jews throughout history).

When I refer to a book of the Bible, I will follow the usual style. For those not sure what that style is, here is an example: Mt 6: 28. The Mt means it is the book of Matthew. The 6 means that it is Chapter 6, and the 28 means it is verse 28. You find verse 28 by looking at the tiny numbers above some of the words. If you look at that verse now, you should be reading Jesus saying something like this: *"And why worry about clothes? Look how the wild flowers grow: they do not work or make clothes for themselves."* Weird. If I didn't worry about clothes, I wouldn't have very much to wear. Maybe Jesus was a nudist.

Anyway, as you'll soon see, there are a lot more references here than just the Bible. And since I want to make sure that you can find the original sources of what I say, I have to make sure to cite my references. Unfortunately, your English teacher is right. You have to cite the places you get your information. Otherwise it will just look like I'm making all this up on my own. Or that I did all the research and want to take credit for it.

But I also don't want the flow of the book to be interrupted with all these references, especially if you don't want to follow up on them right away. So I've come to a compromise. Whenever I say something that you should be able to check for yourself, I will simply put a small number up in the corner of a word, like this.[1] You may already know that the technical name for this number is a superscript. Then if you ever want to follow up and find that source yourself, just turn to the "Notes" section at the back of the book and match your superscript with the number in the notes. There you will find the page numbers and book name of where I got the information. That way, if you don't want to interrupt the flow of the reading, you can just skip right over the number and keep reading. OK? Good.

BC to BCE? AD to CE? WTF?

When writing a book like this, one has to figure out how to represent years. The traditional way is to use the letters "BC"—which stands for "Before Christ," and "AD"—which stands for "Anno Domini," which translates as "In the year of the Lord." The problem is that this is a specifically Christian way of organizing time—the emperor who organized the calendar we use today decided to make the approximate date of Jesus' birth as the start of a whole new way of keeping time. This became known as the year 1 A.D. So in English-speaking historical and archaeological circles, as well as among non-Christians, a new notation has developed. "BC" was changed to "BCE," which now stands for "Before the Common Era." "AD" has been changed to "CE," which, as you have probably already guessed, stands for "Common Era." This is a way to continue using the common dating scheme without implying that it really is "the year of the Lord." I will be using these new initials. Just so you know.

Part One

The Myth of God's Existence

Let's start at the very beginning, a very good place to start.

At the core of Christianity's claims, just like the core of most of the world's religions, is that there exists a being so powerful, so cool, that he (yes, Christianity definitely says "he") created life, the universe, and everything in it. He's so awesome that it is tradition to capitalize the first letter of anything that refers to him. I mean Him. He's so scary and powerful that Jews were forbidden from even pronouncing His real name; they only wrote the letters YHVH.

And yet, ever since there were gods, there have been people who didn't believe in them. Way before Christianity was even a gleam in somebody's eye, the Greeks described the world as being made and manipulated by of a whole bunch of gods that lived on top of a mountain. You know, Zeus and all of them. But the very first philosopher that we know anything a lot about was a Greek guy named Anaxamandros. He dared to describe the world without gods. He thought the universe was a bunch of interconnected cycles that kept itself going without any gods poking their noses in it.[1] So, you can say that the history of humanity is as much the history of skeptics as it is of anything else.

So what do we do today, in the modern Christian era, with this whole idea of God?

Welcome to one of the most hotly debated topics in the history of hotly debated topics. The existence of an all-powerful god who created everything has been argued for literally thousands of years. God's existence has never been accepted by everybody. So there have been many arguments put forth in an attempt to convince people that God is real.

Let's pause here while I explain the use of the word "argument" as it is used in philosophy. Things like the existence of God are explained through logical arguments. This does not mean an argument like a fight, though there have certainly been plenty of those. A logical argument is an attempt to prove something by starting with certain statements, called premises. By accepting the premises, you are led to a certain conclusion. If you don't agree with the premises, or can show they lead to a different conclusion, or have an opposite argument of your own, then you are doing what is called refuting the argument.

The various arguments for God, then, start with different premises that all try to get you to accept the conclusion that God exists. The problem for people today is that the famous arguments can be pretty hard to follow. They were invented centuries ago and written in weirdly complicated ways using language that makes Shakespeare seem easy to understand. Then, as the years go on, other people add other things or responses, so the arguments get even more complicated. It is possible to learn how to read and understand the arguments (it's the basis of many college philosophy courses), but many people today just don't even want to bother. To see what I mean, lets take a look at two of the most often quoted writers used to prove the existence of God, an ancient Greek philosopher and a Catholic philosopher.

Greek philosopher Aristotle wrote one of the first arguments used for the existence of god in his second book of the Metaphysics. It was written in 350 BCE, and this is how he talks (once he's been translated into English):

> Further, the final cause is an end, and that sort of end which is not for the sake of something else, but for whose sake everything else is; so that if there is to be a last term of this sort, the process will not be infinite; but if there is no such term, there will be no final cause, but those who maintain the infinite series eliminate the Good without knowing it (yet no one would try to do anything if he were not going to come to a limit); nor would there be reason in the world; the reasonable man, at least, always acts for a purpose, and this is a limit; for the end is a limit.

Yeah. That's one sentence. What kind of grade would your teacher give you if you turned that in?

The other guy, Thomas Aquinas, was a Catholic philosopher who wrote his proofs of god in the book *Summa Theologica* about 1600 years later than Aristotle. He gave five proofs of the existence of God, though they all had a similar theme. Here is an example of his writing:

The third way is taken from possibility and necessity, and runs thus. We find in nature things that are possible to be and not to be, since they are found to be generated, and to corrupt, and consequently, they are possible to be and not to be. But it is impossible for these always to exist, for that which is possible not to be at some time is not. Therefore, if everything is possible not to be, then at one time there could have been nothing in existence. Now if this were true, even now there would be nothing in existence, because that which does not exist only begins to exist by something already existing. Therefore, if at one time nothing was in existence, it would have been impossible for anything to have begun to exist; and thus even now nothing would be in existence—which is absurd. Therefore, not all beings are merely possible, but there must exist something the existence of which is necessary. But every necessary thing either has its necessity caused by another, or not. Now it is impossible to go on to infinity in necessary things which have their necessity caused by another, as has been already proved in regard to efficient causes. Therefore we cannot but postulate the existence of some being having of itself its own necessity, and not receiving it from another, but rather causing in others their necessity. This all men speak of as God.

So there you go. Did you even finish reading that paragraph? Could you tell that Aquinas felt confident that he just proved the existence of God? He says so in his last sentence. Can you tell that Aristotle and Aquinas were each trying to say the same thing? We'll take a look at what they were actually attempting to tell us in a little bit.

With the way these famous thinkers write about God, it's no wonder people decide to stop trying to figure it out for themselves and just trust other people's ideas about whether or not God exists. But that just doesn't seem fair. Something as important as whether or not God exists should be understandable by everyone! So we'll take a brief look at the four most common arguments for the existence of God, in plain language. Now, while I will make this as easy to understand as possible, it still requires logical thought, so you will probably have to spend some time thinking about it until it makes sense to you.

The Cosmological Argument

For some reason, the most common arguments for the existence of God all have really big and intimidating names. The first one we'll look at is called the Cosmological Argument (which both Aristotle and Aquinas were writing about in those terrible paragraphs above). Aristotle based his argument by looking at motion, and by noticing that things don't start moving by themselves. This fact then forms the main point of the Cosmological Argument. Here is how it goes:

Since everything moves, even the planets, something had to start putting them in motion. Things don't just start moving by themselves. The thing that gave the first "push" is what can be called the "Prime Mover."

Now, this applies to more than just motion. When we look at stuff in the world, we can see that some things cause other things. A firecracker explodes because it is full of gunpowder and lit on fire. Gunpowder is the result of other chemicals mixed together. These chemicals are mixed together because people do it… and so on. This "cause and effect" series also applies to people. You didn't just appear out of nowhere. You were created by your parents. They were created by their parents…and so on.

Everything seems to be caused by something else. The earth itself had to be caused by something. And the solar system. And the galaxy. And the universe. Current science tells us that the universe itself was formed in the Big Bang, which says that billions of years ago, everything in the universe was stuck together in a little dot smaller than the period at the end of this sentence. Then it exploded and eventually caused galaxies, stars, planets, people, and ice cream. And science today can't see what happened before the Big Bang. But if everything has to have a cause, what caused the Big Bang? Doesn't there eventually have to be something that *wasn't* caused by something else? If there is something that caused everything else but wasn't caused itself, it can be called an "uncaused cause."

So, according to the Cosmological Argument, the thing that wasn't caused by something else, the "uncaused cause," was God. God started the Big Bang. And God wasn't created by anything else.

The idea of "God" starting the universe is not unreasonable. But you have to be careful about saying that. If you just say "God" is the name we give to the force that started the Big Bang, it's no big deal. Since we don't know anything about what caused the Big Bang, we don't know anything about God. It's just a word.

Science is getting closer to knowing more about the Big Bang, and there are some theories that say that the Big Bang wasn't really the beginning of the universe, it just seems that way to us from the way we're looking at it. It's very possible that the universe has always existed and never had a start. The scientific theories about all this are too big to fit in this book, but if you're interested, you can read science magazines like *New Scientist*, which publishes articles on the latest research about beginning of the Universe. You can also search the web for things like "imaginary time" and "string theory." But be careful, some of that stuff is hard to understand if you don't know a lot of science already.

Anyway, using the word *God* as a shortcut name for whatever physical process made the Big Bang is fine. But theists aren't OK with just letting "God" be the name for a physical law. They automatically jump from the Big Bang to an actual, intelligent, superhuman force that knows about us and cares about us as individual people. *But there is absolutely no reason to make that jump.* There's a big gap in there that theists just ignore in their desperation to prove that God exists. Science isn't even sure anymore that something caused the Big Bang. And even if something did, we have absolutely no reason to think that that something was intelligent, knew what it was doing, or knows that we exist.

The first argument seems to bring up more questions than it answers. It doesn't seem to lead where theists want it to lead. So lets move on.

The Teleological Argument

The second main argument for the existence of God is called the Teleological Argument. It's also known as the "Argument from Design." This one also seems to make a lot of sense at first. The classic example of this argument goes like this:

Suppose you are walking along and in the dirt by your feet you see a watch. You reach down and pick it up and brush the dirt off and see that it's a pretty cool watch. Now it's obviously not a living creature. It can't have been laying there for hundreds of years. And it obviously wasn't created by accident. It's way too complicated to just have formed by accident. No, it had to have been thought out and designed by somebody. Somebody pretty smart.

Now look around you at the whole world. The world is way more complicated than a stupid watch, so if the watch was designed, that means the earth and the universe were too. The only person that can be smart enough to design everything this perfectly in the whole universe must be God!

Now that sounds pretty good, too. A lot of people go for this idea. But there are some things wrong with it. Can you think of any?

The first thing is that we are *assuming* that the universe was designed in order to *claim* the universe was designed. We have absolutely no idea if universes are the same as watches. We've seen lots of watches and we know how they're made. But this is the only universe we've ever seen; how do we know this fits in the category of "things that are designed"?

The argument from design is the favorite argument of creationists, who sometimes try to make themselves sound scientific by saying they believe in "intelligent design," but all that means is that they don't believe in evolution, they think God created us just as we are today.

But if the universe is designed so perfectly, on purpose, then why do guys have nipples? Females have nipples because they breast-feed babies. Males don't do that. Nipples on guys have absolutely no purpose in life. Why would God design that? Also did you know that all human beings have the remnants of tails at the end of their spines? Sometimes babies are born with actual tails[2] though it's easy for doctors today to remove them. Why would God make kids be born with tails? Interestingly, some Christians used to say that people born with tails were actually children of Satan. So does this mean Satan creates people, too?

Evolution tells us that nipples and tails are features that existed in our ancient ancestors. We evolved from animals that had tails that slowly got shorter and shorter over time until they disappeared. Embryos developing in the womb form nipples before their genitals form—it's just part of the human makeup. But those things, and even more, are still encoded in our DNA and still make their appearances.

Beyond nipples and tails, there are all kinds of things that were "designed" pretty poorly. Like the human eye. The human eye is way more complicated than it needs to be, and even has spots where you are blind.[3] If you think about it, you can probably find other examples of things that were "designed" pretty stupidly. It makes much more sense to say that those things are because evolution is a long and inexact process.

Another way that people present the argument from design is that they will give you all kinds of statistics about how there's no way life could happen without being deliberately created. As a math teacher, I know numbers scare a lot of people. Something about big numbers just makes people shut up and accept what they're told. But don't be fooled.

For example, some creationists like to point out that Carl Sagan, a very famous scientist, once said that the odds against the DNA of a specific person forming randomly and all at once is 1 in $10^{2,000,000,000}$ (that's a 1 with two trillion zeroes after it).[4]

There are a whole bunch of similar numbers that Christians can throw at you. The reason they do that is to make people question evolution. Surely, if it's that rare to get a person to form, maybe there really is a God that made us? It seems that the odds of God existing aren't any worse than the odds are that human DNA would spontaneously appear.

The thing about all those statistics is that they are either taken out of context, so they don't mean what they seem to mean (like the Carl Sagan example), or else they're based on faulty conditions. Creationists don't usually know much science, so they get their scientific explanations wrong. Sometimes creationists will calculate those statistics based on what *they* think, not on what science knows. For example, let's take a closer look at what Carl Sagan said. Does that really prove that evolution can't happen?

The most common mistake about "proofs" like this is that those statistics often ignore what science is actually saying. Christians don't tell you that evolution isn't about things just popping into existence fully formed. It's true that the chances of a full human being just popping into existence right next to you talking about video games are pretty small. But if you were to find where Carl Sagan gave us those extreme odds, and then kept listening to him, you would discover that Carl Sagan didn't believe that DNA did that. *Sagan was using that example to actually explain evolution!* Science tells us that people evolved as a process of natural selection, which is not random, and does not happen all at once. When we understand that evolution happens slowly, a little bit at a time, over millions of years, this greatly increases the odds of life developing.

So the Cosmological Argument is popular today because it sounds very convincing at first. Most people stop right there. But if you actually study it, you realize that people using this argument either don't understand what they are talking about, or are just lying to you.

The Ontological Argument

The word *ontology* basically means "the study of reality." It's a type of philosophy that talks about how reality is structured. The Ontological Argument, then, is an attempt to prove that God exists pretty much because reality demands it. It was first developed by a guy named St. Anselm about a thousand years ago, and is considered an *a priori* argument for God's existence. An *a priori* argument is one that can be proven without going out and finding extra evidence. So what St. Anselm is saying is that you can prove God exists just by thinking about it. That's pretty amazing! Let's see if you are convinced by the argument.

Start by thinking about what the perfect being would be like. Make a list of all the qualities that a perfect being would have. Certainly, whatever else we might expect, we would say the perfect being would be totally good. Not only that, the being would be totally powerful. And it would have total knowledge of everything. We'll call this being "God."

OK, so now we have our perfect being, God, in our head. We want to make sure that God is so great that it's not possible for anything greater to exist. So what's the only thing that can make it the most perfect? Well, existence. Existing is more perfect than not existing. If God doesn't exist, then I can still think of a being that is more perfect than God—one that does exist. But there isn't a being more perfect than God. Therefore, God, as the ultimate perfect being, must exist.

Umm, yeah. Does your mind feel kind of like a pretzel after that one? You might not be surprised when I tell you that this argument is considered the most controversial and weakest "proof" of God's existence.

If you are sitting there thinking, "Yeah, I think I get it. And that's a really stupid proof, but I'm not really sure why," then you are not alone. A lot of people think that there must be something wrong with it, but they just can't put their finger on it. Some people can, however, and there were objections to this argument almost from the time it was first invented.

A guy that was alive at the same time as St. Anselm, by the name of Gaunilo, decided to show that the argument was silly by changing God into an island. Surely, he said, we can think of a perfect island, an island that is more perfect than any other island we can think of. If existence makes something the most perfect, then the perfect island must exist in the world somewhere.

Now, Gaunilo didn't actually believe that a perfect island exists somewhere. He used the idea to show that St. Anselm's proof falls apart. My idea of a perfect island is probably not the same as your idea of a perfect island. Since every person has their own idea of a perfect island, does that mean there is a perfect island that exists for every person on earth? Of course not. The same goes with God. How are we all going to agree on a perfect God?

Other people think the original premises are bad. For example, why is it more perfect to exist than to not exist? That seems kind of random. And why should being "totally good" be more perfect than, say, "totally selfish"? And good for whom? What's good for me might not be good for you.

More than that, if God is totally powerful, we need to define what we mean by power. There is an old logical problem that says, "If God is totally powerful, can he create a rock so heavy he cannot lift it?" If you think about it, either God cannot lift the rock, or he cannot create such a rock. Either way, we've shown that there's something he cannot do. Does that still count as "totally powerful"?

There are other arguments against this proof that take too long to go into here, but you can find them if you are interested in thinking about this more. Besides, since this is an *a priori* argument, you can probably come up with your own way to refute it if you took the time to think carefully.

The Moral Argument

The last argument we will look at is one that is slightly different than the others. It is called the Moral Argument, and tries to show that God exists simply because we have morals. Here is how it works:

People all over the world have some similar morals. For example, no matter where you live, it is usually considered evil to torture a baby for fun. These morals are so common and strongly believed that you can call them facts. It is a fact that torturing a baby for fun is evil. Morals are actually facts; they are commands for people all over the world on how to behave. But if morals are really commands, then there must be a commander. The only commander that can set up morals for all people over the whole world is God. As the Bible poetically says, God wrote the law upon our heart. So God must exist.

This is a clever argument, even if it does seem kind of silly, too. Christians may then challenge those who don't believe in God to explain how people all over the world have similar morals. But it's not really a mysterious answer. You can explain it through instinct and agreements between people.

All animals, from people to mice, have instincts to care for their babies. If such instincts didn't evolve, a species of animal wouldn't try to keep their babies from harm, so they'd be much more likely to die. If enough babies died, the species would go extinct. We can say that we believe that torturing babies for fun is evil because the protective instinct evolved in us.

As another example, take the bigger issue of murder. A lot of people would say that it is a fact that murder is wrong. Just like stealing. But you don't need God to tell us that. People need to agree that such actions are wrong in order to get the benefits of living together in society. Any society that allowed murder and stealing would fall apart pretty quickly. Besides, if you look at how many people murder and steal in the world today (and even torture kids), you would have to come to the conclusion that if God exists, he missed writing the law on a lot of people's hearts!

So those are the main points of the most common proofs of God, and the main points of where the proofs go wrong. Perhaps some of the proofs sounded convincing to you. Perhaps none of them did. There are a lot of places that you can go to learn more about these (and other) arguments. The web is full of them. To be sure, the arguments I described above are not over. Believers and skeptics are still arguing over who is right, and their arguments are getting more and more detailed and logically abstract. But there is still no final answer.

So what does all this arguing prove? Well, it proves nothing. And that's the point. After over a thousand years of debate, *nothing has been proven!* Believers can argue very strongly, but the best they can do is to show that God *might* exit. And even if something called "God" does exist, it doesn't prove what God is *actually like*. So what do you do when you can't prove something?

Suppose someone is on trial for murder. But the lawyers can't prove he committed the murder. Should the jury decide he's guilty anyway? After all, nobody can prove he *didn't* do it. Since he's here on trial anyway, and *somebody* committed the murder, should they just go ahead and assume he's guilty and lock him up? Of course not! So if we can't prove God created the universe, should we just assume he did it anyway? Of course not!

There's a saying that skeptics like to say: "Extraordinary claims demand extraordinary evidence." Which means that the weirder the story, the more proof you need that it is true.

Suppose your friend came up to you and said, "There was a huge dog in my yard last night!" You go over to his house and see large markings in the dirt. You ask him what those marks are and he says,

"Those are its footprints." You ask what kind of dog it was, and he says, "I didn't see it, but I heard it barking." You can even investigate the footprints and compare them to the feet of known types of dogs to find a match. You can even know more about the dog from a description of the bark; bulldogs have very different barks than poodles. You can conclude, then, since wandering dogs in backyards have been seen before, and they do bark, that the evidence suggests that there really was a dog in his backyard last night.

However, suppose your friend came up to you and said, "There was a huge monster in my yard last night!"

You go over to his house and see weird markings in the dirt. You ask him what those marks are and he says, "Those are its footprints." Then you ask him if you saw it make those footprints. He says no.

You ask him what kind of monster it was and he said, "I didn't see it, but I heard it making sounds." You ask him if he can describe it in more detail.

He replies, "No, I told you I didn't see it, but it probably had tentacles, and lots of eyes, because it sounded like something like that would make those kinds of footprints."

So are you going to believe him and tell the cops that there is a monster loose? Probably not. Nobody has ever found a monster in your neighborhood, or anywhere else. Is it possible your friend is right? Yeah, it's *possible*, but if he can't provide real evidence as proof, you're not going to start living your life like there is a monster roaming around your neighborhood.

The claim that the Christian God created the universe is an extraordinary claim. And it has never been proven.

Part Two

The Myth of Jesus Christ

So okay. Even if you are a Christian, really looking at the arguments for the existence of God must show you that atheists have a point. If the arguments were foolproof, there would be no atheists. This is the first place that you need faith, not reason, to believe.

Of course, if we just all accepted the fact that God *didn't* exist, then this book would be finished right now. The whole reason that this book is even written is because a huge amount of people do have that faith and do believe in God, even when they have no real reason to. But Christians go a step or two further than just believing in an intelligent being that created the universe. Christians believe that not only does God exist, but he had a son. A human son whose goal in life was to save humanity. Or at least the Jews, depending on what version of the story you believe. Is faith needed here, too?

What Was up with Jesus, Anyway?

Let's look at the setting of Jesus. The Jews lived in what is still known today as Israel, a country on the Mediterranean Sea, kind of between Egypt to the south and Iraq to the East. The Jews had been living there for a long time, but the Roman Empire had expanded to take over the country and were ruling it. The Jews were afraid that they might not exist much longer as a separate people, so they would sometimes get together and revolt against their rulers. King Herod, who ran things in that part of the country, responded violently to the revolts to keep them down.

Now according to Jewish scriptures (which Christians renamed the Old Testament), a Messiah would someday appear who would drive out the Romans from their country and set up a new Kingdom of God on Earth. The Jewish people were all worked up and ready for this to happen any day. At the time of Jesus (the first century CE), there were a whole bunch of people running around the area, claiming to do miracles, preaching messages of forgiveness and worship, and promising that they were the real Messiah.

What a lot of people don't realize is that the word "Christ" is a title, not a name. It means "Messiah," which in turn means "the anointed one." The Messiah, or the Christ, was someone sent by God to do God's work. The Jews of Jesus' time considered the word even more specifically—the Messiah was sent by God to free the Jews from the rule of the Romans. The title of "Christ" was taken by Christians and pretty much glued to the name Jesus, so we hear about Jesus Christ. Of course, Jesus didn't free the Jews from the Romans, which means that some people—like the whole Jewish religion—say that Jesus was actually not the Messiah because he didn't do what he was supposed to do.

Anyway, the point of all this is that Christ was not Jesus' last name, just a claim to be from God. There were many alleged Christs at the time of Jesus. Actually, we don't know Jesus' last name. The only thing he's called in the Bible is Jesus of Nazareth, which means he came from a place called Nazareth.

Christians, however, will tell you that Jesus was not on earth to free the Jews from Roman rule, that the Jews made a terrible mistake in expecting that. Jesus, according to Christian teaching, was going to save people, all right. But not just the Jews. No, he was out to save all of humanity. And not from physical rulers, but from the sin and misery that was automatically attached to them ever since the time of Adam and Eve.

Talking Snakes and Magical Trees

So let's go back to the very beginning of the Old Testament, the book of Genesis, and look at the story where God created the first two people ever. There are actually two different creation stories, but that isn't important for the connection to Jesus. God created a man that he named Adam, and a woman he named Eve. They were both naked, but they didn't care. They didn't know what being naked meant. They didn't even know good things were different from bad things, because they didn't need to. Evil didn't touch them. God created them, and he placed them in a wonderful garden called Eden. They had everything they needed for a wonderful happy life.

Right in the garden, however, God planted one extra tree. It was a magical tree, because if somebody ate the fruit on it, they would know the difference between good and evil. God didn't want them to have that knowledge. So God planted the tree, and showed Adam and Eve, and told them they could eat whatever they wanted in the whole garden, but they could not eat the fruit that was on this magical tree. So Adam and Eve said okay.

One day, a snake showed up in the garden. It was actually the devil, but he disguised himself as a snake for some reason. He went up to Eve and basically convinced Eve that it wasn't fair that they couldn't eat the fruit of the magical tree. So she went up and ate some fruit and then brought some to Adam and convinced him to eat the fruit too. Right away they gained the knowledge that some things were good and some things were evil. Then they saw that they were naked and got ashamed of their bodies, so they covered up their naughty parts with leaves.

While they were trying to figure out what to do, God showed up and started walking through the garden. Adam and Eve freaked out and went to hide. Walking along, God could tell something was up because he couldn't find the only two humans in the whole place. He called them out. Adam and Eve decided they probably should stop hiding and they came out. God looked at them, saw that they were covering up their genitals, and got them to confess that they ate the fruit of the magical tree.

Well, God was pretty darn mad at that. He threw them out of the garden and set scary angels up at the entrance to the garden with big swords. God told Adam that from now on he'd have to work hard for all food. He told Eve that from now on having babies would hurt.

Christians believe that eating the fruit of the magical tree was the first sin ever committed, and call it the Original Sin. All people born from then on were tainted, dirty, automatically full of sin and therefore unable to get to Heaven. Humanity was doomed.

This is where Jesus comes in. Christians believe that Jesus came to earth to make up for Adam and Eve's original sin. He came to earth to serve the ultimate death penalty. By letting himself be nailed alive to a cross, called crucifixion, he was the blood sacrifice that freed all humanity and let them get to Heaven. His sacrifice counts for all people in all times, even though we don't deserve someone to be that nice to us.

Christians believe that nobody at the time of Jesus expected anything that elaborate. While Jews were expecting their version of the savior, Jesus sort of surprised everybody by announcing that yes, he was the promised messiah, but that he was freeing their souls from sin, not their physical lives from their Roman rulers. So, as we saw, since that's not what the Jews were interested in, they didn't accept him as the messiah. They even thought he was being sacrilegious and insulting to God. So Jesus brought his message to the Gentiles (which just means "people who are not Jews"). Jesus proved that he was right—and the Jews were wrong—by coming back to life after he was killed, and a separate religion formed. A religion, by the way, that historically has never really liked the Jews much.

Pick the Savior!

Now, the following few paragraphs will talk about two figures around at the time. See if you can decide which one became known as Jesus the Christ. If you are someone who was never introduced to the stories of Jesus and don't really know who to pick, don't worry. You'll get a good thumbnail sketch of his life right here.

First, around this time, there lived a man who had the power to heal the sick and raise the dead. He preached messages of love, forgiveness, and how you should worship the one true God. The Romans, who were always afraid of people who might organize people into a large enough group to pose a threat, arrested him and put him to death. After his execution, his followers proclaimed that he had risen from the dead, appeared to them and spoke with them, and then ascended into heaven.[5]

The second figure under consideration was born on December 25. His mother was a virgin when she gave birth to him. He was known as "The Truth," "The Light," and "The Good Shepherd." He preached hope, forgiveness, and immortality, and he came to earth to save humanity from evil. He had 12 followers with whom he shared a last meal, after which he sacrificed himself to redeem mankind. He rose from the dead after three days, and ascended into heaven. His day of worship was Sunday, and by symbolically eating his flesh and drinking his blood, they could attain salvation.[6,7]

If you are like most people familiar with the gospel stories, when you read the first paragraph, you probably decided that he was Jesus. But then, when you read the second paragraph, you changed your mind and thought that the second guy was Jesus, and then you may have wondered why the first guy sounded so similar.

Actually, I tricked you. Neither one of those people was Jesus. The first guy was named Appollonius of Tyana, who died around 98 CE. The second was the Sun God named Mithras, who died way before Jesus was born. In fact the early religion of Mithras provided some very stiff competition for the religion of Jesus. We'll talk more about that later.

So how is it possible for all these guys to be running around doing the same things? Actually, at that time period, there was a basic mythical biography that was attached to great figures—a heavenly figure becomes human while also being the son of a god (apparently, these saviors were always boys). He performs miraculous acts to save mankind and then goes back up to heaven. This story was even applied to Roman rulers such as Caesar Augustus[8] years before Jesus was born. In fact, the ancient writer Celsus wrote about 200 years after Jesus that Christians don't believe in anything new or unusual at all,[9] that it was all said before Jesus arrived. Early Christian writer Justyn Martyr even admitted that was true! However, he argued that everybody else's stories were made up; only *Christian* stories were true.[10] Another early explanation of the stories of previous saviors was that Satan knew that Jesus would come, so he went to all these other cultures and planted false saviors with the same biography that nobody would believe, so that nobody would believe it when Jesus came and it happened for real.

And hey, just like in sports or war, somebody eventually has to win, right?

Even though the story of Jesus may already be looking kind of shaky, it's time now to take a closer look at the details of this miraculous life. After all, if the story of Jesus is actually true, and the New Testament of the Bible is basically his biography, as Christians claim, then we should be able to get some solid proof of it.

As you will see, we do get some proof, all right. But not the kind that Christians want to see.

Putting the Bible in Order

Before we begin examining the Bible to learn about Jesus, it is important to set a few things straight about this book.

When you open a Bible and turn to the New Testament, you will first find the four gospels: Matthew, Mark, Luke, and John. Then you'll find the Acts of the Apostles, and then a whole bunch of letters, called epistles, most of which were supposedly written by a guy named Paul; but there are a few others written by other people as well. And then finally is a really trippy book known as Revelations.

And since that's the order the New Testament is presented, that's the way people read it. And like most books, people will keep in mind the earlier stuff as they read the later stuff.

And that's where a big problem is. Because the order of the books in the New Testament is *not* the order in which they were written. And the "authors" of the gospels weren't the guys whose names are attached.

According to most scholars[11] the first things written were the epistles of Paul, who wrote them between 48 and 62 CE. Then, around 70 CE came the gospel of Mark. 15 years later came Matthew, who pretty much just copied Mark and added a few extra stories and changes[12]. Soon after that Luke also used Mark as his source, and changed a few more things. He also wrote the Acts of the Apostles as a sequel to his gospel. Then around the year 100, John came along and wrote his gospel, which was totally different from the other three guys.

Now, if you look at it in that order, you'll find some really interesting things. Paul wrote first, the closest to Jesus' death, but he doesn't mention anything about Jesus' actual life. He keeps talking about Christ and his resurrection and visions he had, but he never says this was Jesus of Nazareth, or mentions any miracles, or anything. Along comes Mark who says a few things, but keeps his story pretty sparse. Then the others write their books, and each one adds more and more miraculous and fantastic happenings. The further away from Jesus we get, the more legendary he becomes. It's sort of like Elvis. Even though he died in 1977, people today are telling stories about how he faked his death and how he's really alive somewhere. Legends sort of naturally spring up around people.

But I don't want to get too far ahead. Let's start studying Jesus as far back as we can go. And for us, we can go back to a curious list, a record of Jesus' relatives before he was born.

Jesus' Fractured Family Tree

The Old Testament prophets predicted that the Messiah would be a descendent of king David, one of the most famous figures in the Jewish scripture. So surely, then, if the story of Jesus was actually true, there would have to be some record of descendants from David to Jesus. All we would have to do is count how many "great" grandfathers there were between David and Jesus. And sure enough, the Bible does include a record of Jesus' family tree. Well, actually, there are two records. And they, uh, don't match.

The first chapter of Matthew lists 42 generations between King David and Jesus, starting with David's son Solomon, and ending with Jesus' grandfather Jacob, who gave birth to Joseph, who was Jesus' father. But the third chapter of Luke also gives an account of Jesus' lineage. And he says that there were 76 generations, starting with David's son Nathan and ending with Jesus' grandfather Eli. And most of the names in between don't match with each other, either. Hmm.

Of course, Christians learn that Mary was a virgin when she gave birth to Jesus; she had never had sex with Joseph. So if that was true, why would there need to be a family tree? Jesus would not have been descended from David anyway.

Who's Your Daddy:
The Not-So-Virgin Mary

One of the most interesting traditions of the beginnings of Jesus' life is the belief that his mother, Mary, was a virgin. But this story doesn't seem so clear-cut, either.

Remember that Mark's gospel was written first, about 40 years after Jesus died. His gospel mentions nothing about Jesus' birth or childhood. His gospel starts when he is already an adult. Matthew was the next gospel written, and he says that Mary was a virgin. He proves this by quoting from the OT (Mt 1:22) about a virgin becoming pregnant and having a son. However, Matthew was quoting that text in the Greek language, and the word "virgin" was there. But the original language, Hebrew, does not say "virgin." It simply says "young woman."[13] The Greek translation made a mistake. So, it is entirely possible that the whole virgin birth story was based on a mistake.

In fact, many early Jewish Christians totally rejected the idea that Jesus was born of a virgin because that story was used in so many pagan legends of heroes, including Plato, Alexander, Perseus, and many others.[14] So almost from the *very beginning* there were people who thought the virgin birth was already an overused myth.

Certainly, any real evidence that exists definitely suggest that Jesus was born the old-fashioned way. What's even more interesting is that in the early days of Christianity, Jews were spreading the idea that Jesus was actually the love child of Mary and a Roman soldier named Panthera.[15]

The Birth of Jesus

The story of the Nativity, or the birth of Jesus, is so famous that many non-Christians know it. In a nutshell, this is the story: In the country of Israel there was a nice Jewish carpenter named Joseph who was engaged to a nice Jewish lady named Mary. Angels announced to Mary that she was going to have a baby. The fact that she hadn't slept with Joseph yet (after all, she wasn't a slut) didn't matter, because the real baby's daddy was God. When Joseph found out his fiancée was knocked up, and he knew he wasn't the father, he wanted to quietly break things off with her. Luckily, an angel appeared to Joseph in a dream and explained the real deal.

The emperor Caesar Augustus made a declaration that said that everyone in the whole empire had to go to the town where their parents were born and register for a census so that they could be taxed. Joseph and Mary were living in a town called Nazareth. But Joseph's roots were in a town called Bethlehem, which was about 70 miles away. So even though Mary was going to give birth at any time, he loaded her up and they traveled to Bethlehem.

When they got to Bethlehem, they tried to check themselves into an inn to stay. But the inn was overbooked, and there wasn't any more room. So Joseph found a stable where the cattle and sheep were kept, and they settled down there. That's where Mary one night had her son, who was named Jesus.

As Jesus was born, wondrous things happened. Angels appeared in the sky and started singing to shepherds, telling them about how God just had a son, who was sleeping with farm animals. And a mysterious new star appeared in the sky, which was noticed by three kings from countries away, who traveled to Israel to see what all the fuss was about. They go to see King Herod and ask him where they can find the new King of the Jews. Herod had no clue, so he asked his advisors. His advisors said that the new King of the Jews was in Bethlehem. King Herod is pretty upset at all these new developments, because he doesn't want anybody going around claiming to be the new king. He wants to find out exactly where this kid is, so he can kill him. So he tells the three kings to go find the child, and when they're done worshiping him, to come back and tell him where the child is so he can go worship, as well.

So the three kings set off for Bethlehem. On their way, an angel appears to them telling them that they should definitely not go back and tell Herod where Jesus is, they should go back by another route. The kings arrive to find the child, and here is our typical Nativity scene; three kings giving gifts to a baby surrounded by hay, with gentle farm animals quietly looking on and shepherds in pious poses.

OK. Before we go on and look at the rest of Jesus' childhood, let's take a look at this story. Because while this is the story we have, it is not written that way in the Bible. This story comes from combining and tweaking a couple of different Bible stories. In order to fully understand the birth story, we'll need to look at each part of the New Testament separately.

As we have seen, the first New Testament literature written was Paul. He wrote the closest to the life of Jesus. What's Paul's story about the birth of Jesus? Well, nothing. He never mentions the birth or childhood of Jesus. He must not have thought it was that important. Or else he never heard of it.

OK, fine. The gospels are the main source of Jesus anyway, let's see what Mark's gospel says about the birth of Jesus, since it was the first gospel written.

Well, Mark's gospel starts when Jesus was an adult. There was no birth story given by Mark, either. Now that you mention it, when you begin looking at the other gospels, we see that John also never mentions it. All we have left are Matthew and Luke.

Ok, fine. Matthew and Luke have the story of Jesus' birth. Let's look at each one of them separately.

Matthew's story is pretty short. It tells the story of Joseph finding out Mary was pregnant and all that drama. Then it jumps to saying that Jesus was born in Bethlehem, which they were already living in. Then it says that sometime after the birth (it doesn't say how long), some astrologers were following a star and came to Jerusalem and asked where to find the king of the Jews. King Herod got very upset at this news, and the whole city of Jerusalem was upset too (we don't know why the whole city would be upset). He asks his advisors about it. His advisors consult the Old Testament and find a scripture that suggests it would be Bethlehem (which, if you read that OT scripture—Is. 7: 14-16—it becomes clear that it really has nothing at all to do with Jesus. Matthew made a huge mistake in trying to make it a fulfillment of a prophecy[16]). The rest of the three kings story follows from there.

So that's Matthew's account. What about Luke's story? Well, Luke's story talks about the census, and the stable, and the angels and shepherds. It does not mention the three kings or King Herod.

So Matthew says a "star" led the kings to Jesus. Now let's think about that. What kind of star would lead someone to an exact house? Stars are huge balls of fire like the sun, not little magical fireflies. Besides, if they were following a star, why would they need to stop at Herod's house and ask directions?

Furthermore, considering they were from another country (Matthew says they were from the East), and they couldn't just hop on a plane and fly to Jerusalem Airport. They had to walk and ride camels. How long would that take? How long would Jesus have to sit in a manger among cow and sheep dung waiting for these kings to give him presents? In fact, Matthew doesn't know anything about a stable or a census at all. He never says that the family actually went anywhere. This is an important point that will mean something a little later.

Meanwhile, Luke doesn't mention any star at all, but somehow simple shepherds could walk to the town of Bethlehem and find him right away. And Matthew doesn't know anything about shepherds or angels.

OK, so the two stories seem a little shady. Surely history will help us out.

Actually, history pretty much kills the whole thing.

History books written at the time also make no mention of appearances of angels, weird stars, or upset cities at the idea of a new king being born.

Matthew's gospel says the whole birth thing happens during King Herod's reign. Well, according to contemporary history books, Herod died about the year 4 BCE. So Jesus had to have been born sometime before that. But Luke's gospel says Jesus was born during a census taken when Quirinius was governor of Syria. The history books of the time put that census at about 6 CE. That's ten years *after* Herod died![17] So either one—or both—of those accounts must be false.

Now, if this was an ordinary biography of an ordinary man, such questions and uncertainties may not bother us too much. Someone made a mistake somewhere. It's not a big deal. But this is no ordinary man. And the Bible is no ordinary book. It's supposed to be the inspired, true Word of God. So you think God would at least get the story of the birth of His only son straight. But he doesn't. His family tree is a mess, there is no evidence that Mary was actually a virgin, and they can't even be sure when the man was even born!

Already, even at the birth of Jesus, we have seen contradictions in the inspired Word of God that cannot be reconciled. At least part of the Bible has to not be literally true. And unfortunately for Christian literalists, it gets worse from here. But before we continue, let's take a closer look at what we call Christmas today.

The Real Christmas Story

Every December, among the Christmas trees and dreams of Santa, we hear that the true "reason for the season" is the story of the birth of Jesus. After all, the name "Christmas" literally means the "mass of Christ." However, in actuality, the reason for the season has nothing at all to do with Jesus.

Apparently, despite the angels and miraculous star, nobody actually knew the date that Jesus was born. By the second century, there were a number of arguments about when the special day was. There were reports that it was on May 20. Some said April 20. Some said November 17, others said March 28. There was a large group that stubbornly celebrated Christmas on January 7, and who still do.[18] Apparently, God never stepped in and straightened things out.

By 354 CE, the date of Jesus' birth was set at December 25. However, that was not because things were finally settled. Historians believe that Church authorities set December 25 as the date because it was already being celebrated as the birthday of Mithras.

Who was Mithras? Great question. He was a Sun God, and was worshipped through worshipping the sun. December 25 was considered to be his birthday because that corresponded closely to the winter equinox, when the days begin getting longer again.

The cult of Mithras had some other interesting things about it. Mithras was believed to have been born of a virgin. He was known as "The Good Shepherd," and preached hope and mercy. He had a close group of twelve men around him, and sacrificed himself to save mankind. He descended into the underworld and three days later rose from the dead.

Many scholars believe (though it is contested by some Christian scholars) that the cult of Mithras influenced the development of the legends surrounding Jesus. Certainly, there are too many similarities to be a coincidence. In fact, some sects of Christians (which still exist today) accused the December 25 believers of actually participating in sun worship.[19]

So if the date isn't specifically Christian, what other Christmas traditions have Christian roots? How about the Christmas tree? Or the Yule log? Or Holly or mistletoe?

Let's see. A little research (which is widely available) tells us a lot. The Christmas tree comes from pagan traditions of using the evergreen tree to symbolize the renewal of life. The Yule log comes from a Germanic Norse tradition of sun worship. During Yule (which corresponded to the winter solstice), male animals and human slaves were sacrificed by suspending them from tree branches. Holly was sacred to Celtic druids. Mistletoe was important in Norse mythology. Yule was also the origin of the giving of presents, and the Norse god Wodin provided some seeds of the origin of Santa Claus. The traditional colors green and red are said to be pagan colors representing life and death.

Certainly Christianity has come up with their own explanations and uses for these traditions. But is there anything about Christmas that is specifically and originally Christian? Well, there is. The name. But that's about it.

The Child Jesus Leaves
Dead Boys Behind

OK. So Jesus, the Savior of the Universe, was born as a boy somehow, at some time, even though we're not exactly sure how, or when. So what happened next? Well, the answer to that, like most things in the Bible, depends on what book you read.

Luke depicts Jesus childhood as fairly normal; Chapter 2 talks about how Jesus was circumcised and presented in the Temple like all first-born Jewish males were. The young Jesus meets a couple of people who proclaim him the savior, and then they return to their hometown of Nazareth.

Matthew doesn't give Jesus such a happy early childhood. In Chapter 2, after the kings left the baby Jesus, an angel appears to Joseph and warns him that Herod will be looking for Jesus to kill him. Joseph is supposed to take his family to Egypt right away. Not just to another town where Herod isn't looking, but to a whole new *country*. It must have been an emergency because Joseph and Mary got up in the middle of the night, bundled up the baby Jesus, and ran off to Egypt.

Meanwhile, King Herod, just like the angel said, realizes that the kings from the East weren't coming back to tell him where Jesus was. So in what can only be described as the ultimate overreaction, he sends orders to kill every boy in Bethlehem and the surroundings who was 2 years old or younger. Not just babies, mind you, but everyone up to 2 years old. This is the famous incident known as the "slaughter of the innocents." Of course, Herod was foiled, because Jesus was far away.

After King Herod died, an angel appeared to the Mary and Joseph once again and told them to return to Israel. So they headed back towards Bethlehem, where they lived. But then they heard that Herod's son Archelaus was now ruling Judea (where Bethlehem is located), and they didn't want to go back there. So Joseph had yet another dream that told him to take his family to Nazareth and live there (here it's good to notice another contradiction—while Matthew says that Jesus' family moved to Nazareth only when they decided their home in Bethlehem was unsafe, Luke said they had always lived in Nazareth and were just visiting Bethlehem when Jesus was born).

Now that's quite an adventure that Jesus was supposed to have had, especially since Luke said nothing like that happened. Which story is true? Let's check the history books. There are biographies of King Herod, written during and after his reign, books that do list terrible things he did. But there is no record anywhere of any slaughter of children. Something like that would have made history. So it certainly appears that Herod's famous mass murder just didn't happen.

Not only that, but Matthew tells us Joseph was afraid to return to Bethlehem because Herod's son was in power. Well, another of Herod's sons, Herod Antipas, also ruled Nazareth, where Joseph wanted to go. According to logic, then, Nazareth was no safer than Bethlehem.[20]

Matthew justifies all these weird stories by saying that old prophets had foretold the Messiah coming from Egypt and being called a Nazarene. The only problem with that is that there were no such prophecies.[21] Despite being "divinely inspired," it is clear that Matthew is just plain wrong. Wrong about history, wrong about prophecy.

So anyway, besides one other story from Luke about how Jesus was found teaching in the Jewish Temple when he was twelve, his life is a completely missing from his early childhood to his baptism at around 30 years old. Despite being such an Ultimately Important Historical Figure, nobody thought to write anything about him while growing up.

Well, unless you consult one of the gospels that wasn't allowed in the Bible.

The Other Gospels

When people think of the gospels, they usually think only of the four in the Bible, the ones that we have been speaking of. But history has left us with many more than that. Scholars have found the texts of around 40 other gospels, written by many different people. None of these gospels were accepted into the final version of the Bible that we see today, but they do exist.

Some of those other gospels do carry stories of Jesus; stories that present Jesus in a very different way than we are used to. One of the most famous of such stories tells how Jesus, as a little kid, went out into the street one day and saw children playing. Jesus went to follow them, but they ran off and hid. Jesus came to a house where women were standing and asked them where the children were. The women said there was no one there, and Jesus asked who was hiding in the furnace, knowing it was the children. The women said it was only a few goats. So Jesus turned the children into goats and wouldn't turn them back until the women begged for mercy.[22]

Other, weirder stories, exist[23]:

While Jesus was supposedly in Egypt, he confronted dragons.

When Jesus was five, he made 12 sparrows out of clay by a brook, brought them to life, and sent them flying away. He watched the water of the brook flowing by, gathered the water into a small pool, and commanded it to become clean, which it did. Another boy came by with a stick and splashed the water away. Jesus then cursed the boy, who completely withered up.

While walking through the village, another boy ran by and knocked his shoulder. Jesus was irritated and killed him right there. When some of the parents complained to Joseph that his son was killing the village children, Joseph got mad at Jesus and asked him why he did things that made the village hate them. Jesus reassured his father, saying he knew that other parents were making Joseph yell, so he wasn't mad. And he cursed the complaining parents, who immediately went blind.

These are only a few of the legends that sprung up around the young Jesus. There are numerous accounts of him raising the dead to life and performing other miracles, all as a child.

Now, nobody thinks these stories are true; they are simply legends of the type that often spring up when there isn't any real biographical data. However, we are supposed to believe the miracles of Jesus' later life, though they are just as unbelievable.

Jesus the Miracle Worker

So nobody seems sure of anything about the Savior of the Universe's birth or childhood. It's not until he's an adult and makes a sudden appearance at the river Jordan that we see some similarities. All the gospel stories have an account of Jesus' baptism by John. Now, that doesn't mean that all the stories match, exactly, but at least they all agree that he was baptized. This baptism starts the public life and preaching of Jesus, which lasts for an undetermined amount of time, but which is usually guessed at either one year or three years, depending on which gospel you're reading. Anyway, during this time Jesus preaches and performs miracles and generally causes a huge stir. The Jewish leaders think he's blaspheming (which means seriously insulting God) by calling himself God, and the Roman rulers are nervous that he'll lead a rebellion against the empire. This adds up to his arrest and execution.

I won't spend a lot of time going over the details of Jesus' public life, though it's not because there's nothing to say. It's just that getting into the details requires a much deeper examination of how the Old Testament was completely reinterpreted to make it mean things it never was supposed to mean, in order to fit accounts of Jesus' miracles. It would also be necessary to do a study of ancient literary styles. While it is an interesting topic, it is a lot more academic and technical than this book needs. It also doesn't have much of an effect on discovering the truth about Jesus. If people want to believe that Jesus performed miracles, well, I can't stop them.

There are a few things we should notice about this phase of Jesus' life, however.

First, as mentioned earlier, there was nothing special about the miracle stories. A lot of people had similar stories attached to them. For that matter, some of the miracle stories have an uncanny resemblance to miracle stories of religious figures from other countries. For example, there is a story in Matthew of Jesus walking on top of a lake to reach his disciples and helping one of them get out of the boat to stand on the water too. That story was already being told about Buddha, who lived way before Jesus did.

Second, the gospel writers apparently had very poor knowledge of geography. These authors who supposedly lived during the life and times of this great man made many mistakes about where things were. They would have failed a geography test about their own land, but they supposedly were good biographers.[24] Similarly, they made mistakes about parts of Jewish law that everybody knew at the time.[25]

Jesus' Crucifixion
and Resurrection

So let's look now at what the ultimate point of the Christian faith, the crucifixion and, most importantly, the resurrection of Jesus. And if the stuff earlier in this book makes literalist Christians uncomfortable, then they need to make sure they never, ever read this part of the Bible. Unlike the birth story, Jesus' miraculous resurrection is recounted by all four gospels. Unfortunately for Christians, they each tell a different story.

Let's start our investigation on the morning of the resurrection. Who were the first people to arrive at Jesus' tomb?

Mark (at the beginning of Chapter 16) says that Mary Magdalene, Mary, the mother of James, and Salome went and found that the huge stone that was placed over the entrance to Jesus' tomb had been rolled away. That's three women.

Luke says [24:10] that Mary Magdalene, Mary the mother of James, Joanna, and some other women went. They saw that the stone had rolled away from the entrance to the tomb. So here we have at least 5 women, including Joanna instead of Salome.

Matthew says [beginning of chapter 28] that it was just Mary Magdalene and "the other Mary" who arrived at the tomb, which was still blocked by the large stone. But suddenly there was a violent earthquake, and an angel came down from Heaven, rolled away the stone, and then sat on top of it.

John says [beginning of chapter 20] that Mary Magdalene went all by herself, saw that the stone had been rolled away, and ran off to tell a couple of apostles that somebody stole Jesus' body.

Are you keeping track? Depending on which gospel you read, there are anywhere from 1 to 5 or more women. The condition of the stone also does not match from story to story.

Continuing on, what did the women see when they arrived at the tomb?

Mark says the 3 women entered the tomb and saw a young man wearing white. He told the women that Jesus had risen from the dead and was on his way to Galilee. He told the women to go tell the disciples to meet Jesus there. Then the women, who were terrified, ran away and didn't tell anybody what they saw.

Luke says that the 5 or more women went into the tomb and found it empty. Then two men in shining clothes appeared beside them and told them that Jesus wasn't there, that he had come back to life. The women ran away to tell the disciples, but the disciples thought the women making stuff up. Peter went by himself to see the tomb and saw the empty grave cloths.

We left Matthew's story at the point where the two women had felt the earthquake and saw an angel roll away the stone. The angel looked like lightning and spoke to the women—who weren't inside the tomb. The angel told the women that Jesus was alive and going to Galilee, and that they should go tell the disciples. On their way back, Jesus appeared to the ladies and told them not to be afraid. The ladies told the disciples, who set off for Galilee to meet Jesus.

Back to John, Mary Magdalene told Peter that Jesus' body had been taken away. Peter and another disciple ran to the tomb and went inside, but found nothing except the burial cloths. Then they went home. Mary apparently stayed at the tomb alone, because John says she was crying, and then she looked into the tomb and saw two angels in white who asked her why she was crying. She said somebody took away Jesus body and she didn't know where it would be. Then Jesus, disguised as a gardener, asked Mary what was wrong. Mary told him, and he called her name. She recognized Jesus, who told her he had come back to life. Mary ran to tell the disciples what happened.

Let's try to make some kind of a summary here. Mark and Luke don't agree on the number of women who went to the tomb, but agree that they found an empty tomb and did not meet Jesus. Matthew said the women met Jesus. John said that Mary Magdalene alone met Jesus, but it was later, on her second trip to the tomb. And she thought he was a gardener.

So when and where did the risen Jesus meet the disciples? Mark stops his story after he says the women were too scared to tell anybody. Matthew says the disciples found him on a hill, where they worshipped him and Jesus told them to go out and spread the word to all people everywhere. Luke says Jesus appeared to the disciples in Jerusalem, and told them not to go anywhere until God gives them power. John says the disciples were in a locked room, not a hill, when Jesus appeared to them.

Again, if the resurrection of Jesus was an actual historical event, destined to change the direction of the entire world, and the Bible was literally true, inspired directly by God, there would be some agreement as to when and where Jesus appeared to his biggest fans and told them to spread the word. But there's not. Jesus appeared either in Jerusalem, on a hill in Galilee, or in a locked room somewhere.

A Brief Note on Jesus, Rabbits, and Eggs

Have you ever noticed that while Christmas is the same day of the year every year, December 25, Easter is not? It's always on a Sunday, but it can be anywhere from March 22 to April 25. The date of Easter is calculated as being on the first Sunday after the first full moon after the spring equinox. This method of calculating the date stems from ancient pagan religions that scheduled their holidays according to phases of the sun and moon.

There were many pagan religions that celebrated the death and resurrection of a god/man around the time of the spring equinox. One of the most common was the god Attis, who was worshiped around 500 years before Easter became associated with Christians. According to tradition, he was born of a virgin, and then died and resurrected at the end of March.

The name "Easter" is itself pagan. It is hypothesized to come from the name Ostara (sometimes spelled Eostre), a Germanic goddess of fertility and sex, which were often celebrated in the springtime. Rabbits are famous for their ability to have sex and give birth to large litters of baby rabbits. Eggs are obvious symbols for fertility and birth. All of the symbolism of Easter is about sex and birth (or rebirth) and are way older than the story of Jesus rising from the dead.

Similar to Christmas, then, the Easter traditions are generally considered to have been a Christian attempt to absorb older holidays when Christians moved into and began converting non-Christian lands.

Jesus in History

Anyway, back to the main topic. It seems that God not only can't get his story straight about his only son's birth, but He's also fuzzy about the single most important event in world history. Well, maybe there are other books and records that exist, real historical documents, that can shed some light on the situation.

Many scholars have spent a lot of time to find specific, concrete, proven references to Jesus as a historical figure. Here's a summary of what they've found:

Nothing.

But OK, let's be fair and look at what Christians will tell you when you say this. They will almost certainly bring up the ancient historian Flavius Josephus. He was a Jew who at first led a revolt against the ruling Romans. However, he was captured, and soon decided that fighting the Romans was hopeless. So he switched sides and became an interpreter for Rome. He went on to write huge histories of the life and times of the people before and during the time of Jesus.

Remember, it is widely known that at the time of Jesus, there were a whole bunch of people proclaiming themselves to be "messiah," running around performing miracles and pronouncing that believing in God would bring about the freedom of the Jews. Such men Josephus noted included Judas the Galilean, Theudas the Magician, and an Egyptian guy that Josephus never named. All of these men were condemned by Josephus, because all their teachings were contributing to the unease and sense of revolt among the Jews, which Josephus had left behind.

But apparently, Josephus knew about Jesus, as well. The most important reference to Jesus is a paragraph which is now called the "Testimonium Flavian." Here is what the paragraph says:

About this time there lived Jesus, a wise man, if indeed one ought to call him a man. For he was one who wrought surprising feats and was a teacher of such people as accept the truth gladly. He won over many Jews and many of the Greeks. He was the Christ [Messiah]. When Pilate, upon hearing him accused by men of the highest standing among us, had condemned him to be crucified, those who had in the first place come to love him did not give up their affection for him. On the third day he appeared to them restored to life, for the prophets of God had prophesied these and countless other marvelous things about him. And the tribe of Christians, so called after him, has still to this day not disappeared.

Well, that sounds pretty convincing, doesn't it? Especially given Josephus's hatred of other "messiahs" of the time, why did he like this Jesus guy? Was it because he was all he was cracked up to be?

Not really. What most Christians who quote this paragraph don't bring up is that that it is pretty much every scholar admits that it was forged. First of all, Josephus never mentions Christians again in the whole book. That's all there is.

Also, remember that back in those days, there was no printing press. Every book had to be copied by hand. It would be extremely easy for the copier to add in stuff he wanted the book to say. Scholars have subjected that paragraph to many studies and comparisons, and all of them generally agree that the paragraph was inserted into the text a couple of hundred years after Jesus' death.[26] While some Christian scholars try to argue that some sentences in the paragraph might be real, even they admit that a lot of it is forged.[27]

So Christians will often point to another important historian, Tacitus. Although he lived some time after these events, he is famous for one paragraph about the Christians. His comment takes place at the time that the capital city of Italy, Rome, was burned, and there were rumors that the ruler Nero started it:

To suppress this rumor, Nero fabricated scapegoats— and punished with every refinement the notoriously depraved Christians (as they were called). Their originator, Christus, had been executed in Tiberius' reign by the governor of Judea, Pontius Pilatus. But in spite of this temporary setback the deadly superstition had broken out afresh, not only in Judaea (where the mischief had started) but even in Rome. All degraded and shameful practices collect and flourish in the capital.[28]

Scholars here agree that Tacitus did actually write this paragraph; it is authentic. One of the reasons it is considered authentic is because Tacitus openly hates the Christians; he calls them "notoriously depraved" and calls their religion a "deadly superstition." But the fact that Tacitus knew that Christians existed doesn't really tell us much. All he really says is that some dude named "Christus" was killed, and Christianity grew. This doesn't mean it was Jesus of Nazareth, who rose from the dead.

The other few instances in history books that people claim are about Jesus are vague references to "Christ" or "Chrestus," and we have to remember that Christ was not Jesus' last name, just a general word that meant Messiah. There were many people at the time calling themselves that.

There were other historians of the time, ones that lived close to Jesus, including Plutarch, Seneca, Martial, Quintilian, and Epictetus, among others. But not one of them mentioned one word about Jesus. Not one word. For someone who fed 5000 people with a few loaves of bread, who raised people from the dead, cured people, and even resurrected himself after dying, you would think that would get some kind of mention. If that doesn't get you into history books, then what will?

So to sum up, our knowledge of Jesus is contained in one fake paragraph, some vague references to messiahs of the time, and Bible stories that already contradict each other so much that we know that some or all of them must be fiction. In other words, using common sense and rational thinking, we can see why atheists (or even the followers of other religions) believe that the life of Jesus is mostly, if not completely, made up. Christians are perfectly free to believe it all, but the point is that they are relying on *faith*, not reason.

Part Three

The Myth of America's Christian Origins

One issue that is very important to many people, especially atheists, is the idea of "separation of church and state." Coming from the First Amendment to the Constitution, the idea basically states that when you have a place or organization that is run by the government, then you can't let that place or organization support any one religion. This is because the government is supported by taxes that are paid by everyone. It's not fair for Christians to give money to the government if the government shows favoritism to non-Christian religions. However, it's also not fair for non-Christians to give money to the government if the government supports Christianity.

One of the big battlefields over this issue is public school. Many lawsuits and fights have started over whether or not kids can be forced to listen to prayers in school. Or whether clubs can form (like for gay and lesbian kids) if those clubs offend Christians.

Other legal fights happen over government buildings. There have been lots of lawsuits over whether or not the Ten Commandments can be posted in government buildings, since the Ten Commandments are a specifically Jewish and Christian document.

I was talking with a friend one night about my retreat from Christianity. I had thought that he would be supportive, for during high school I was much more religious than he was. I was surprised to find out that during the time we didn't talk much, he had been "born again" as an ultraconservative Catholic. He immediately began to yell at me, saying that atheism cannot be true because it is a recent development, and certainly didn't exist back when America was started. He believes that the whole idea of "separation of church and state" was made up by atheists to attack religion, and that the founders of America didn't mean to keep religion out of government.

I knew he was wrong, and told him so, though it didn't do any good. I soon began to understand that a lot of conservative Christians believe that atheism is new. In their desperate claims to show that the country is faithful to Jesus, they are also desperate to re-write American history as a Christian adventure. They proclaim that from the very beginning, America and all the main players (like George Washington, Thomas Jefferson, and Benjamin Franklin) were Christian. And they are hoping that you will just take their word for it. But what will you find if you don't just take their word for it, and look into it on your own?

Was America Founded
as a Christian Nation?

In 1779, just three years after the Declaration of Independence and still years away from the Constitution, Thomas Jefferson thought up a bill in his home state of Virginia that he thought was important for the emerging independent states. His Bill was called the Act for Establishing Religious Freedom. It was his idea that religious leaders and rules should stay completely away from the government. Jefferson said he "meant to comprehend, within the mantle of its protection, the Jew and the Gentile, the Christian and Mahometan, the Hindoo, and infidel of every denomination."[29] This meant he thought that the government should protect every person, no matter what religion they did (or didn't) have.

Of course, it wasn't a completely easy sell, and seven years of debate followed, but in 1786, a version of Jefferson's original bill passed. There were a few revisions, in order to satisfy everyone, but it was enacted essentially how Jefferson wanted it. One of the biggest changes was the opening sentence; while Jefferson opened the wording with a salute to reason before an acknowledgment of God, the final bill opened with the words "Whereas, Almighty God has created the mind free…" [30]

However, before people start claiming that that the lawmakers were good Christians, it must be noted that those lawmakers overwhelmingly *rejected* a motion to honor Jesus Christ. Instead, they went with the more general "God." This rejection of the authority of

Jesus was just what Jefferson wanted. As he said later, that proved the law was meant to protect everyone, Christians, non-Christians, and non-believers, as well[31]. Actually, the law itself was designed to remove the common requirement that in order to hold public office, a man was required to say they believed in God. Here is the actual wording of the important part of the law:

> *Be it enacted by the General Assembly of Virginia that no man shall be compelled to frequent or support any religious worship, place, or ministry whatsoever, nor shall be enforced, restrained, molested, or burthened in his body or goods, nor shall otherwise suffer on account of his religious opinions or belief; but that all men shall be free to profess, and by argument to maintain, their opinion in matters of religion, and that the same shall in no wise diminish, enlarge, or affect their civil capacities.*[32]

In today's words, the law can be paraphrased like this:

> "It's now a law that in Virginia, nobody has to belong to any church or religion at all, and nobody should be hurt or discriminated against because of their religious opinion; everybody has the right to their own religious views and it will not affect anything they want to do for public office."

So much for Thomas Jefferson (or the Virginia legislature) wanting a Christian nation.

Virginia's religious freedom act was instantly news over in Europe, because it was so bizarre. That had never been done before. The text was immediately translated into various languages in Europe so that other countries could read the new ideas of religious freedom themselves. Of course, the European governments, who united government and religion, were not happy. But individual people got really excited at the idea of making something like that work in their own countries.

So if the idea of religious freedom was so important to Jefferson, what were his personal beliefs? Was he a Christian?

Thomas Jefferson was very interested in the topic of religion. But when he talked to people about the subject (usually in written letters), he would ask them to not tell anyone what they talked about. He knew his ideas were unusual. For example, while he was the president, he took a razor to the New Testament, and actually cut out all the parts that he thought were unbelievable. Then he reordered the Bible into something that made more sense to him. Today this book is known as the *Jefferson Bible*, and it is still being printed today.

However, even though Jefferson was secretive about his beliefs, he did write one book in which he pretty much gave himself away. The book was called *Notes on the State of Virginia*, first published in 1785 in France. In it he says, "It does me no injury for my neighbor to say there are twenty gods or no god; it neither picks my pocket nor breaks my leg." He was against establishing official churches and. forcing religion on people because "millions of innocent men, women, and children, since the introduction of Christianity, have been burnt, tortured, fined, imprisoned..." and doing those things has not done any good toward making everyone one religion.[33]

Not only did Jefferson's personal ideas make him pretty unpopular with many preachers of the day, but so did his friendships. Jefferson had a personal friendship with Thomas Paine, who first became famous by writing the pamphlet "Common Sense," which inspired many to fight for their freedom from England. After the war was over, however, he wrote a book called *The Age of Reason*. The book was entirely dedicated to getting rid of organized religion and replacing it with reason and the laws of nature. Paine declared that:

> Every national church or religion has established itself
> by pretending some special mission from God,

PAUL DONOVAN

communicated to certain individuals. The Jews have
their Moses; the Christians their Jesus Christ, their
apostles and saints; and the Turks their Mahomet, as if
the way to God were not open to every man alike.
   Each of these churches show certain books, which
they call revelation, or the Word of God. The Jews say
that their Word of God was given by God to Moses; face
to face; the Christians say that their Word if God came
by divine inspiration; and the Turks say that their Word
of God (The Koran) was brought by an angel from
heaven. Each of these churches accuses the other of
unbelief; and for my own part, I disbelieve them all.[34]

   The book was instantly controversial, and preachers everywhere
began preaching about how Paine was evil. Some Christians began to
say that Jefferson was really not fit to help run the country because
he was friends with Paine.
   Even so, the book was a bestseller and was reprinted multiple times
because the book kept selling out.
   Given how famously important Thomas Jefferson is in American
history (after all, he was the main author of the Declaration of
Independence and the third president of the United States), he isn't
really the example that conservative Christians are trying to tell us he
was.
   Unfortunately for those Christians, it gets worse.

84

Deism

So anyway, if the mention of "God" in Virginia's law didn't really mean the Christian God, what did it mean? That's an interesting question, and one that conservative Christians try to ignore. To get to the answer we need to go back a few years, to the founding of the country itself.

Remember that the original American colonies were settled in part by people who were being persecuted for their religion in Europe. Puritans, Calvinists, Lutherans, Presbyterians, Quakers, Baptists, there were many small religious groups, usually called "sects," which came to America because they didn't agree with the main religious strands in their home country. They felt that they had to go somewhere far away so they wouldn't be bothered. So from the beginning there were many different, even competing, religious views settling in the new land. A lot of them were different types of Christians, but there was a growing number of other views, as well. One of the most important early American people who had one of those other views was Benjamin Franklin.

Benjamin Franklin was born in Boston in 1706. However, he left that town as a teenager partly because, as he said, he wasn't quiet about the fact that he doubted Christianity, and people began to point and gossip about him that he might be an atheist.[35] He also later recalled that when he moved to Philadelphia, on his first day there he went to church in a Quaker meetinghouse... and fell right to sleep.[36]

Franklin was not actually an atheist, though his religious beliefs amounted to the same thing in the minds of most people around him. When he was fifteen years old, he had decided Christianity was false. Then he ran across some books on Deism, and soon counted himself a Deist.

Most people today haven't heard much about Deism, and it is a general term that can be interpreted in somewhat different ways. For the purposes of this part of history, however, Deists can be summarized in a few important concepts[37]:

1. Deism believes in a god, but that's it. Nothing else.
2. The deistic god is also known as the "clockmaker god," in that at the beginning of time, God created the universe and then stepped back and doesn't have anything else to with it. This is usually illustrated as the idea of a guy constructing a clock, winding it up (or plugging it in), and then just stepping back and watching it without doing anything else.
3. Deists think that evidence of God does not come from the Bible, which they didn't believe was holy or inspired by God. For deists, evidence of God comes from nature, and how wonderfully it was designed. Remember the Teleological Argument we talked about earlier? They would have pretty much agreed with it.
4. Deism rejects organized religion as well as the idea that God gave people all the answers so that all we have to do is obey Him.
5. Deists usually thought that Jesus was a wise man, but was not the son of God, did not raise from the dead or save mankind.
6. Deism supports reason, logic, and experiment. It believes that answers to questions can be found through science and reason, not through asking God for the answer.
7. Some radical deists even believed that Christianity *prevented* moral improvement and social justice.

If you think back to the beginning of this part of the book, you might suspect that not only was Benjamin Franklin a Deist, but so was Thomas Jefferson. And you would be right. And in the 1750's deism was gaining popularity. It was spreading enough that the more traditional Christian leaders were getting alarmed. Deism was equated with atheism, and was to be beaten down.

However, Deism was becoming so popular that the Founding Fathers (those men who were responsible for putting together the basis for the United States) used deistic thought as the background on which to construct the new American government. This growing connection between religious free thought and political freedom was so obvious that conservative ministers were anxious to separate them.

A lot of people were against the conservative ministers. Ethan Allen, a famous Revolutionary War hero, wrote a book called *Reason the Only Oracle of Man*. In it, rejecting the idea of an all-powerful God, he noticed that God seemed to run the world a lot like the terrible kings back in Europe. He wondered why that was, especially since those kings were the reason they left their homelands in the first place. He also said that priests loved the idea that people need God to know what to do, because if people were able to figure things out for themselves, the priests would be out of a job. More than that, Allen believed that while the priests ruled things, they would always fight reason and nature so that they could make up other rules.[38] The book caused a stir and the president of Yale University said that the book was "the first formal publication, in the United States, openly directed against the Christian religion."[39] And this was before the Constitution was written.

From the very beginning of the nation, Christian denominations were trying to find ways to get a foothold. Back in Virginia, where the battle over Jefferson's law of religious freedom was going on, there was another proposed law that would put a tax on everybody in the state, so that the money could be used to pay people who taught Christianity.

Another of the Founding Fathers, James Madison, thought that the proposed tax law was a terrible idea and made a speech saying so[40]:

If Religion be not within cognizance of Civil Government, how can its legal establishment be said to be necessary to Civil Government? What influence in fact have ecclesiastical establishments had on Civil Society? In some instances they have been seen to erect a spiritual tyranny on the ruins of Civil authority; in many instances they have seen the upholding of the thrones if political tyranny; in no instance have they been seen the guardians of the liberty of the people. Rulers who wish to subvert the public liberty, may have found an established clergy convenient auxiliaries. A just government, instituted to secure and perpetuate it [liberty], needs them not.

Paraphrased in today's language, the above paragraph basically says:

If the government doesn't need to pay attention to religion for its laws, why does government need to legally support religion? What does religion do for society? Well, sometimes it destroys civil government and becomes spiritual bullies; lots of times religion supports unfair and terrible kings; religion has never been seen to guard people's freedom. Any ruler who wants to destroy public freedom can find that religion will help them do that. Any fair government intending to secure and spread freedom does not need religion.

The speech was very well received and eventually signed by two thousand citizens of Virginia, which was a lot of people in the new state. Again, this is not exactly evidence of a Christian America.

What is really interesting about this proposed law of using tax money to support Christian churches is that it was only supported by the largest denominations, mainly Episcopalians. The much smaller, evangelical churches like Baptists, Quakers, Methodists, and Presbyterians, all agreed the tax law was bad. This was partly because they didn't want to let the Episcopalians get even more power, but also because being evangelical meant that the real relationship between people and God was personal, and uniting church and state was not only unnecessary, but an insult to God as well.[41] Today's evangelicals don't quite see it that way anymore.

America Grows Up—
Without Dependence on God

Imagine a family (perhaps like yours) with a child that has reached about 18 years old, and is ready to move out and make his own life. Imagine that his parents aren't ready for him to declare his independence, and a fight begins. Anybody that has been through such a struggle knows that it almost never ends well.

On a bigger scale, that's what happened with the United States. The colonies founded by England eventually got fed up with their British overseers and declared themselves independent. So the British declared war in order to keep those ungrateful Americans in order.

The Declaration of Independence in 1776 is like a letter that the newly-adult child writes to his unaccepting parents explaining that he's now independent and that he's moving out and wants them to stay out of his business. No laws were formed or proposed in the Declaration of Independence, there was nothing in it that set up the newly independent states as a country in itself. Conservative Christians are eager to point out several references in the Declaration that point to God, though again, there is no mention of the God being specifically Christian.

Of course, somebody moving out of their parent's house is fine, but that doesn't automatically mean that the newly-independent adult automatically knows what to do next in the big world. The same goes for a newly-independent country. So a few years after the Declaration, in 1781, the Articles of Confederation were written and accepted, which were the first tentative steps for all these new states to organize themselves. The Articles proposed the name The United States of America, and were an attempt to loosely gather the states together without making too much of an actual government—everyone was still too mad at the repressive government they just escaped from to try to make another whole system of telling its people what to do.

In another vague phrase, the Articles of the Confederation acknowledge the goodness of "the Great Governor of the World." These Articles would soon be replaced by the actual Constitution of the United States, which must be an embarrassment to all who attempt to prove the Christian origins of this country.

Finding God in the Constitution

In 1787, the work began to create an official Constitution that would permanently serve as the basis of the government of the United States. By this time, states had their own constitutions, and the search was on for one of those states to use as an example, a model to base the nation's constitution on.

Among the choices to use as the best model[42]:

- Massachusetts. This constitution extended equal protection of the law, and the right to hold public office only to Christians. And not just any Christians; Catholics weren't included unless they took a specific oath saying they wouldn't listen to the pope.
- New York State. New York extended equality to Jews, but not Catholics.
- Maryland, which guaranteed full civil rights to Protestants and Catholics, but no Jews, deists, or freethinkers. The only Catholic signer of the Declaration of Independence, Charles Carroll, never even considered giving civil rights to non-Christians.
- Delaware, which required all public office holders to publicly swear that they believed in the Trinity.
- South Carolina, which actually established Protestantism as the official state-sponsored religion.

It is obvious that Christianity (and arguing about Christianity) was well established among the people of the early nation. However, the framers of the Constitution picked none of these states as the model for the national document. The state they picked for the model was Virginia. Remember Virginia? The state that officially declared religious freedom was best, including atheism. That's the one that the founding fathers wanted to base America on.

So if the Declaration of Independence used the terms "God" and "Creator," and the Articles of Confederation used the term "Great Governor of the World," what religious term was written into the Constitution?

Nothing.

There is not one mention of God in any way in the entire document. This was not an accident; it was a deliberate use of language that was immediately noticed by the more conservative Christians in the states. Not only that, but the Constitution also included a rejection of a religious test, like Virginia's (Article 6, section 3). It stated that anybody who wanted to hold public office "shall be bound by Oath or Affirmation, to support this Constitution; but no religious Test shall ever be required as a Qualification to any Office or Public Trust under the United States." This meant that the only thing that the government official had to swear was that he would obey the Constitution, but he didn't have to agree to any religious belief to get the job.

Writing the Constitution, however, didn't automatically mean that it was accepted by all the states. No, each state had to ratify it individually. And that's where the battles began.

A North Carolina minister, attending the state debate on whether to accept the Constitution, said that without a religious test, the Constitution basically amounted to "an invitation for Jews and pagans of every kind to come among us."[43]

More than the rejection of religious tests, however, some Christians were outraged that the Constitution deliberately omitted a mention of God. New York Reverend John Mason predicted that if American citizens didn't show more religious respect than was found in the Constitution, that God would "overturn from its foundations the fabric we have been rearing, and crush us to atoms in the wreck."[44] Similar doomsday prophecies emanated from other pious folk.

There were, during the long process of state-by-state ratification of the Constitution, many attempts to change the Constitution into declaring that the nation's power comes from God or Jesus. However, every one of those attempts was defeated. Through all the dire warnings and religious bigotry, the majority of Americans liked the secular Constitution—and not just atheists and freethinkers. Like the tax question in Virginia, many smaller religious sects, distrustful of powerful and established churches, feared being crushed if religion was officially allowed in government. More than that, many people of faith genuinely believed that faith is an individual matter, and not something that needed to get mixed up in government.

Well, history tells us what happened. The purposely non-religious Constitution, the basis of all law in the country, was approved and ratified. Not only that, but the First Amendment to the Bill of Rights in 1791, known as the establishment clause, officially put into words "Congress shall make no law respecting an establishment of religion or prohibiting the free exercise thereof..." which has angered and thwarted conservative Christians ever since.

The New Nation Becomes Even Less Christian

Once the Constitution was put into place, other states, whether newly admitted to the Union or already established, also began to support religious freedom in their constitutions:

> • Kentucky, the fifteenth state, was admitted in 1792. Evangelical Christians and non-religious people formed a majority and established separation of church and state.
> • South Carolina and Georgia, between 1789 and 1792, also removed all religious conditions from their constitution.
> • Delaware got rid of its requirement that officeholders had to swear that they believed in the Trinity, but they still had to swear that they believed in God and heaven and hell. This allowed Jews to hold office, though not atheists.

Connecticut and Massachusetts, however, remained staunchly religious states with direct connections between church and state. This bothered both Thomas Jefferson and Henry Adams. Jefferson even said that both of those states were "the last retreat of Monkish darkness, bigotry, and abhorrence of those advances of the mind which had carried the other states a century ahead of them."[45] In

1818, when Connecticut finally broke off the state establishment of the Congregationalist Church, Jefferson wrote Adams that he was very happy that "this den of priesthood is at last broken up, and that a protestant popedom is no longer to disgrace the American history and character."[46] It wasn't a complete victory, however—Connecticut would not give equal rights to Jews until 1843. And it wasn't until 1833—after Adams died—that Massachusetts would remove religious discrimination from its laws.

Even the first president of the United States, George Washington, had no intention of making America a specifically Christian nation. He wrote a letter in 1790 to the Jewish community in Newport, Rhode Island, in which he said, "For happily the Government of the United States, which gives to bigotry no sanction, to persecution no assistance, requires only that they who live under its protections should demean themselves as good citizens… May the children of the Stock of Abraham, who dwell in this land, continue to merit and enjoy the good will of the other inhabitants, while every one shall sit in safety under his own vine and fig tree, and there shall be none to make him afraid." [47]

Since George Washington was America's first president, he has been the subject of many efforts by today's religious leaders to make him seem like a devout Christian. However, the evidence really points to him being a Deist, too. Most scholars today believe that stories of Washington's strong Christianity are made up. Even religious leaders who personally knew Washington testified that he never knelt at prayer. [48]

Pirates and Muslims
and Christians, Oh My!

For about three hundred years, there were Muslim nations in North Africa that controlled the Mediterranean sea lanes that countries needed to use to trade stuff with Mediterranean countries. These nations, called the Barbary Powers, controlled the seas through piracy—they would attack ships and capture the people, who either became slaves or hostages. Many countries just paid bribes to the Barbary Powers to leave them alone.

Early America needed to trade with the Mediterranean countries, as well, and the Muslim pirates also captured American sailors. This was supposedly partly done in an attempt by the Muslims to capture Christian sailors to get revenge for the Inquisition, in which the Christian church tortured and killed Muslims for not being Christian.[49]

America did not yet have a navy, so fighting the pirates really wasn't possible. Like many other nations, then, America agreed to pay off the Barbary Powers. In 1796 a peace treaty was written up and read to the United States Congress, which unanimously approved it. It was signed and put into place. The full text of the treaty can be found online,[50] but what makes it famous is Article 11, which states:

> As the government of the United States of America is not in any sense founded on the Christian Religion—as it has in itself no character of enmity against the laws, religion or tranquility of

96

Musselmen [Islam],-*and as the said States never have entered into any war or act of hostility against any Mehomitan* [Muslim] *nation, it is declared by the parties that no pretext arising from religious opinions shall ever produce an interruption of the harmony existing between the two countries.*

Read that first sentence again. Right there, in plain English, is the phrase "the government of the United States of America is not in any sense founded on the Christian religion…" the rest of the paragraph explains that since America is not founded on Christianity, America doesn't hate Muslims, so there's no religious reason to start a war.

Some Christians today are trying to make excuses for this treaty, such as that Congress approved the treaty quickly because they were too busy to argue over minor details.[51] However, if Christianity was so important to the government, it's hard to believe that the statement "The government of the United States of America is not in any sense founded on the Christian religion…" would hardly be considered a minor detail.

A lot of Christians that actually do know about this treaty seem to admit that yes, the treaty is a statement that the government was not founded on Christian principles, but that there were still a lot of Christians in America.[52] Well, duh. Nobody has ever argued that there were no Christians in America. The myth is not that America was entirely atheist. The myth is that that America was founded on Christian principles. It is a myth that history has shown to be completely false.

"Under God" and "In God We Trust"

If we move ahead in history, we'll find another favorite topic that believers claim as proof that America is a Christian nation—the words "under God" in the Pledge of Allegiance, and the phrase "In God We Trust" printed on American money. However, as you might suspect by now, things are not what they seem. Let's take a brief look at those two issues.

The Pledge of Allegiance was written back in 1892. The National Education Association (which still exists today) wanted something that all children could say in school all across the country, to show how all children, from many different countries, can come together as one people in America. The pledge was written by Francis Bellamy, who was a former Baptist minister. Though Bellamy was a Christian, he was also a socialist and strongly believed in the separation of church and state.[53] He wrote the Pledge of Allegiance like we know it today… except for one thing. His last line was "one nation, indivisible, with liberty and justice for all." He did not write "under God." The pledge was illustrating how all children were united as a country, not as a religion. At the beginning, the pledge was only recited in public schools—private religious schools would not use it because it did not mention God.

Over half a century later, in 1954, the Pledge of Allegiance was changed to include the words "under God" in the last sentence. It was put in as a way to distinguish America from its new enemy, Russia.

People everywhere were afraid of communism, which was associated with atheism. So, in order to show that America was better than Russia, the Pledge was altered to include a religious statement. So people that say the Pledge of Allegiance proves America's government is supposed to be Christian either don't know their history, or are lying to you. The phrase "under God" was added decades after the pledge was written, and for more political reasons than religious ones.

Similarly, the motto "In God We Trust" also did not start with the beginning of the country. It started during the Civil War, when both the North and the South each claimed that God was on their side. During this time, which showed a great increase in religiosity, the government began receiving requests to acknowledge God somehow on money. It was debated and worded and re-worded, and in 1864 the phrase "In God We Trust" was placed on pennies and the two-cent coin.

In the decades after the civil war, the phrase was sometimes put on some coins, and sometimes not; if you are a coin collector, you can find old coins where the motto is missing, such as nickels from 1883 to 1938. In 1908 the coins were standardized to include the phrase on all new coins.

In 1956 (two years after the phrase "Under God" was added to the Pledge of Allegiance), Congress decided to adopt the motto "In God We Trust" as the national motto. The old motto was E Pluribus Unum, which meant "Out of many, one," which matched the intent of the original Pledge of Allegiance. E Pluribus Unum has not disappeared, you can still see it around, but it "officially" now isn't as important as saying that all Americans trust in God.

So yes, Christians are right in pointing out the Pledge of Allegiance, the national motto, and coins. But they are wrong in saying it was always like that. Just because it happened before we were born doesn't mean it was that way from the beginning.

Part Four

Life Without God: Myths About Being Atheist

Like many groups of people, there are a lot of stereotypes and myths about atheists. And like most stereotypes, they are based on a lack of real knowledge about the subject, so outsiders just fill in the blanks with their own fears and prejudices. It has happened to groups of various races, genders, and sexual orientations. It certainly also happens to people of various religions. And, perhaps especially, to people of no religion.

This section of the book will deal with the biggest myths that I and most atheists have encountered in our daily lives as we try to live life freely in a society dominated by Christianity. Like most stereotypes, each person has to deal with them individually, so this section of the book will contain the largest amount of personal opinion; I certainly can't speak for every atheist when answering these questions. However, a lot of atheists answer these stereotypes, these myths, in similar ways. And like most stereotypes, you will see that they really don't hold up when looked at closely.

Myth #1: Atheists Have No Morals

Not too long ago, I was working with a guy who was a "born again," ultra conservative Christian. We were talking about our experiences as teachers helping inner-city youth, and he suddenly looked at me very strangely. He knew that I was atheist, and he asked me, "If you don't believe in God, why do you help people? Why do you do good things?"

At first I thought he was kidding. But no, he was deadly serious. So I looked him in the eye and said, "It's called human compassion." He looked at me like I was some sort of strange bug that he couldn't understand. But it's true. Despite what Christians might want you to believe, human compassion is a natural part of being alive, no matter what religion you are. It's not just Christians that think that murder is bad.

It's a common stereotype that people become atheists for selfish reasons. Supposedly, we want to be atheists so that we can live life as selfishly as we want without feeling guilty about it. I used to believe that one myself, when I was a Christian. But as I grew, I met atheists who were nicer than a lot of Christians I knew. And as I began to let go of my faith, I realized just how wrong that stereotype is. It's true that sometimes atheists will come to a different moral decision than Christians. Some Christians will then say that to have "different morals" from theirs equals "no morals." It's a very ignorant and arrogant thing to believe.

The fact that Christianity makes a big point of morality means that many people think that Christianity invented it. Surely, many

Christians like to believe that. But that is actually pretty ridiculous. Any study of the other religions in the world will show many religions that have similar rules for treating others with respect. OK, fine, Christians say, but the Bible has all the good ideas about how to live, so we should all just get our moral system from the Bible, right?

That belief leads to one of the biggest problems that Christians have with atheists—without a book to guide them, how are they going to know what's good and evil? How are they going to know how to behave themselves? Christians get their morals from the Bible itself, which comes from God, so it can't be wrong.

Well, we've already talked about the idea that the Bible can't be wrong. And it is true that atheists use logic and their moral intuition to decide what counts as good and evil. But is it true that Christians really depend strictly upon what the Bible says so that they stay consistently within the commands of God?

Not really.

The Morality of the Old Testament

The Old Testament, as a record of how Jews are supposed to live, have plenty of rules for us to follow. Here are some of them. This is how we are supposed to lead our lives, according to God:

- If you work on Saturday, you will be killed.
- If you go to a psychic for advice, you will be killed.
- If you curse your parents, you will be killed.
- If you are gay, you will be killed.
- Stay far away from shrimp, clams, oysters, lobsters and crabs.
- If you are blind, handicapped, have a flat nose, or are a dwarf, or have an itching disease, or scabs, or crushed testicles, you can't go near the altar of God.
- If your son disobeys you, you can kill him.
- If a man rapes an unmarried virgin, he has to pay her father some silver and then marry her.
- Women who are having their period cannot go to church or even be looked at because they are unclean.
- If you are a woman, your words only count if your husband or father says so.
- You cannot touch the skin of pig.
- You cannot wear clothes made of more than one type of thread.
- If a husband suspects his wife is cheating on him, he can make her drink poison. If she lives, she is innocent. If she dies, then she was guilty.

• If a man discovers on his wedding night that his wife is not a virgin, he is supposed to take her to her father's doorstep and kill her.

• You can beat your slaves (male or female), but if you knock out an eye or a tooth, you have to let them go free.

• If you beat your slave (male or female) and the slave dies right away, you will be punished. But if your slave does not die for a day or two, then you're all right.

Not only are these rules silly and cruel, but a number of them are actually illegal! But this is how the Bible says we should live. This is the book that Christians hold up as the guide to life.

Ah, but you might be thinking, that's not fair. What about the Ten Commandments?

I'm glad you asked.

The Ten Commandments

In America today, the Ten Commandments get a lot of attention. Not only in churches, but among people who want to display them in government buildings and other public places. People fighting for the public display of the commandments say it is out of respect for the religious founding of our nation (which I already covered in the last section of the book), and because they form the basis of American law. Something that important deserves a closer look, don't you think?

Many people think they know the story of the Ten Commandments, but it is highly likely that they only have been told part of it. The story, and the adventures surrounding it, is recounted in the book of Exodus, and it goes like this:

Moses was a guy that God picked to go to Egypt, because the Egyptian pharaoh had kidnapped all the Jews, who were has favorite people in all the world. The Jews were a group of thousands and thousands of people, divided into twelve smaller tribes, who lived in a land called Israel—that's why they were also called Israelites. Anyway, Moses went to Egypt and told the pharaoh that he wanted to leave with the Israelites. The pharaoh refused, so God made terrible things happen to the Egyptians until the pharaoh told Moses he could have the Israelites back. So they all left and spent the next 40 years wandering around the desert, waiting for God to tell them where to stop.

About 3 months into this desert journey, Moses and the Israelites stopped at a mountain called Sinai. Now, God would only talk to Moses, and He told Moses to tell the people that he had something big and important for them, so they should stop having sex and go get cleaned up and be ready for the big announcement. God said he was going to come down to the mountain to talk to Moses, and Moses should set up a boundary around the whole mountain that nobody should cross. If somebody touches a foot upon the mountain, everyone needs to stay away from him and throw rocks at him or shoot arrows at him until he's dead.

So the Israelites got themselves ready and they waited for God to come down. After three days there was a loud trumpet blast, and thunder and lightning appeared, and a huge cloud came down spitting fire and rested on the top of the mountain. It was God. He sat there for six days; and on the seventh He called Moses up to the top of the mountain to give him something. Moses went up and stayed at the top of the mountain for 40 days and nights while God told him all kinds of things about how to act. God then gave Moses two tablets made out of rock which contained the basic rules that the Israelites must go by. These were the Ten Commandments.

Let's pause the story right here (because, contrary to what you might think, the story is not over yet), and list the Ten Commandments, which are supposed to be the basis of American law and morality. There are different minor translations between Bibles, and for some reason, the Jews, Catholics, and Protestants put the commandments in slightly different order. But this is the list that is generally accepted:

> *1. I am the Lord your God. Thou shalt have no other gods before me.* [Translation: "I'm your God. Don't go worshipping anybody else."]

> *2. Thou shalt not make a graven image.* [Translation: Don't make or keep any statue or picture of any god.]

> *3. Thou shalt not take the name of the Lord thy God in vain* [Translation: "Don't say things like 'God damn it' because it's disrespectful. Don't disrespect God."]

4. Remember thou keep the Sabbath Day
[Translation: "Don't work on Saturday because it's holy." God explained that the reason for this was that's the day God rested after He created the world, so everybody should rest too. Christians later changed the Sabbath to Sunday.]

5. Honor thy Father and thy Mother. [Translation: "Obey and respect your parents. Don't be a pain to them."]

6. Thou shalt not kill. [Translation: "Don't kill anyone."]

7. Thou shalt not commit adultery. [Translation: "Don't have sex with anyone other than your husband or wife."]

8. Thou shalt not steal. [Translation: "Don't steal."]

9. Thou shalt not bear false witness against thy neighbor. [Translation: "Don't tell lies about people." This includes gossip.]

10. Thou shalt not covet thy neighbour's wife. Thou shalt not covey thy neighbor's house, animals, or goods. [Translation: "Don't wish you could have sex with somebody else's wife, and don't wish you could have the stuff that other people have."]

Curiously, the Catholic version of the commandments doesn't count Number 2 as a commandment, and instead breaks Number 10 into two parts. Anyway, let's take a look at these and see if they really are the basis of all morality and law in the United States.

As author Sam Harris notes,[54] the first four commandments really have nothing to do with morality at all. They are more like rules for dating. Basically, God is saying, "Let's be together, but only under these conditions." Over and over again in the Old Testament, God admits he is a jealous guy, and if he finds his people are cheating on Him with other gods, he gets really angry and starts killing. Kind of like an abusive boyfriend or husband.

So are there laws in America connected to these commandments? Can you get arrested for not worshiping God, or having a statue of Jesus, or swearing, or working on Saturday? No, you cannot. It's insane to even propose.

Commandment 5 is a generally good idea (unless the parents are abusive or something like that), and can be considered moral, I guess. But can you get in trouble with the law for thinking your parents are morons? Again, no.

Commandments 6 and 8 are the ones that do have laws based on them. But so does every country I know of, Christian or not. Those are definitely not specifically Christian values.

Commandments 7, 9, and 10 are moral rules, but again, there's no law against any of them (unless you lie under oath during a trial).

So we have Ten Commandments, only about half of which are really rules about morality, and only two of which have laws attached in America. Honestly, other than 6 and 8, how much of a basis is the Ten Commandments to American law?

By the way, it has been shown[55] that the commandments like "Thou shalt not kill" also don't mean what people today think it means. It specifically applies only to how Jews should act toward other Jews. It means that Jews should not kill other Jews. If one is not a Jew, then you can kill them. This explains a lot of the stories later in the Bible when the Israelites went and killed lots of people of other nations (like the story of Joshua at the battle of Jericho). And other passages in the Bible referring to one's "neighbor"—like "love your neighbor"—also only applies to Jews. So technically, Commandment 6 doesn't apply to anyone who isn't a Jew.

Anyway, let's get back to our story of Moses and the Ten Commandments, shall we? Because here is where it gets *really* interesting:

So while Moses was up on the mountain for a month and a half, all the people were down below and they were getting bored and worried about what happened to Moses. So they went up to Aaron, who was in charge while Moses was away, and said, "We don't know what happened to Moses, so let's make up a new God to lead us."

Aaron then had everybody take off their gold jewelry, and he melted it down and made a statue of a bull calf. And everyone said, "Here is God! He got us out of Egypt!" And they decided to have a party, which turned into an orgy of alcohol and sex.

Meanwhile, God figured out what was going on at the bottom of the mountain, and he got really, really mad and was ready to kill them all. But Moses told God he was overreacting and that he should calm down a little. So God changed his mind, and Moses went down the mountain with his two stone tablets that had the Ten Commandments on it.

When Moses got to the bottom of the mountain he saw the gold statue and the people partying, and he got so mad he threw the Ten Commandments on the ground and they broke. Then he took the gold statue, melted it, and ground it up into powder. He mixed up the powder into water and made everybody drink it. Then he yelled at Aaron for letting this happen. Aaron said, "It's not my fault, you know how bad these people are. They wanted a new god, so I told them to take off their gold jewelry and I threw it all in the fire, but out of the fire came this gold statue!"

Moses moved to the entrance of the camp and called for everyone who was still loyal to God to come join him. One of the tribes, called Levites, came to join Moses. Moses told the Levites, "God wants you to go through the camp and kill all your friends, your sons and brothers, and your neighbors with your swords." So the Levites did that, killing about 3000 men and boys that day. After it was all over, Moses told the Levites, "By killing all those people, you have shown your service to God, so he blesses you; you are now priests."

The next day, Moses told the people, "I'm going to go back up the mountain and see if I can get God to forgive you." So he went up and talked to God and asked him to forgive the people. God told Moses to lead everyone away from the mountain and continue their journey. Then he sent a disease down to kill more people.

By now, the people were pretty miserable and sorry. God told Moses to tell everyone that he would show them where to go and settle, but that God wouldn't go with them because he would probably just kill them all on the way. But if they stopped wearing jewelry, God would think more about what to do. So all the people stopped wearing jewelry.

Moses set up a tent wherever they went so that he could talk to God. God would come down in a pillar of cloud and enter the tent and talk with Moses like two men. Eventually Moses talked God into going with them to the land He promised them. Moses was very happy and asked God if he could see God's real face. God said no, because anyone that sees God's face automatically dies. But God said he could put Moses into an opening of a rock and put His hand over his face so that he could at least see the back of God. Eventually, after Moses got done talking with God, his face would "shine" so that everybody was afraid to go up to him. So Moses put a cloth over his face and wore it everywhere so people wouldn't be afraid of him.

God told Moses two make two more stone tablets and he would re-write the Ten Commandments on them, since Moses broke the first set. So then Moses had another brand new set of the Ten Commandments.

Now, what a lot of people don't know, even if they do know that God gave Moses a second set of commandments, was what the second set of Ten Commandments said. Everyone is taught that they were just a copy of the original commandments. But they weren't. According to Exodus, Chapter 34, this is the second set of Ten Commandments:

1. Worship only God: Make no agreements with the inhabitants of other lands to which you go, do not intermarry with them, and destroy their places of worship. [This was basically the same as the original Commandment 1, with some extra stuff]

2. Do not cast idols. [This is basically the original Commandment 2]

3. Observe the Feast of Unleavened Bread for seven days in the month of Abib [This was the Passover holiday, where all Jews go to Jerusalem to commemorate the final plague that God sent to the Egyptians]

4. Sacrifice to God the first male animals born. The first male donkey born may be saved, and you can save firstborn sons.

5. Do not work or even make a fire on the seventh day of the week. Anyone who does so will be put to death.

6. Observe the Feast of First Fruits and the Feast of Ingathering: All males are therefore to appear before God three times each year. [These are two more holidays, related to harvest times].

7. When you sacrifice an animal to Yahweh, don't include any bread that doesn't have yeast in it.

8. Do not keep any part of a sacrificed animal overnight.

9. Bring the best of the first grain of the harvest to the Temple of God.

10. Do not cook a goat in its mother's milk.

So yeah. Although nobody seems to know it, the Ten Commandments we know were actually replaced by the ones just above. Apparently the best way to keep God happy is to sacrifice animals and have holidays. Never mind things about being good to people. Oh, and mass murderers can become priests.

So that's a brief look at the Old Testament. I could go on and on with stories like heroes of the Bible that offer their daughters for rape, or have incest, but that would make the book longer than I want. Feel free to continue this research if you want; for now I'm sure you get the picture.

New Testament Morality

Here, Christians will always say, "Well, sure but Jesus and the New Testament changed all those rules anyway." This can be taken care of quickly. Actually, no, Jesus didn't change the rules. There are times in the New Testament (such as Matthew 5:18-19) where Jesus specifically says he doesn't want to change one bit of the Old Testament. And Paul, in his second letter to Timothy, states "All Scripture is inspired by God and is useful for teaching the truth, rebuking error, correcting faults, and giving instruction for right living." Hmm. Not exactly what the Christians are telling us.

Yes, of course, Jesus did preach what we know basically as the Golden Rule: Do to others what you want them to do to you. That is an undeniably good, moral rule to follow. But the thing is, he wasn't the first one to come up with it. There were lots of teachers that taught that rule hundreds of years earlier, like the Buddha and Confucius. It wasn't a new idea even in Jesus' time.

In addition to that, Jesus said that if any man wanted to follow him, he had to "hate" his father, mother, wife, kids, brothers and sisters, and even his own life (Luke 14:26). The New Testament specifically calls on women to obey their husbands. Paul believed that women should not speak in church. This means women should not sing in church choirs, teach Sunday school, or even participate in church services. More than that, if a woman ever wanted to learn something, she should just ask her husband at home.

So the final answer that many Christians will offer is "Well, we've moved on from those days. It's obvious that our sense of morality has evolved since those days. Not all those rules apply anymore." And that's exactly my point. Everyone, Christian or not, decides for themselves which rules are appropriate for living. There is nothing in the Bible that says "You have to obey this one, but this one doesn't apply anymore." The Bible doesn't provide a strict guide for *anybody*, atheist or not, and hasn't for a long time. We decide what parts of the Bible are good and which are not. We know that the Golden Rule is good, and we know that killing your disobedient son is bad, even though the Bible says they're both good.

The fact that there are so many Christian denominations shows that the morality of atheists isn't even the big issue. All the different Christian religions have their own interpretations of the Bible, and have their own ideas of which rules to live by and which ones they can ignore. Everyone is on their own.

The biggest example of the struggle to decide what parts of the Bible to accept and which to ignore comes in the issue of slavery.

The American civil war lasted so long because there were many Christian churches (mostly in the south) who pointed to the Bible as proof that slavery was OK. For example, in the book of Exodus, God gives these rules:

• You can buy male and female slaves from countries around you.
• You can buy slaves from strangers traveling through your land.
• The slaves are your property, and you can put them in your will to give to your sons after you die
• You can sell your daughter to be a slave, but if her master doesn't like her, she gets to go free.

And of course, we've already seen that you can beat your slaves as long as you don't knock out an eye or tooth or kill them right away.

In the New Testament, Jesus never says slavery is bad. And Paul says that slaves should obey their masters just like they were obeying Jesus. And in his first letter to Timothy, Paul also says that slaves should treat their masters with total respect, especially if their masters are Christian; slaves should actually work harder for their Christian masters because the Christians benefit from the slaves' work.

While there were definitely Christians that found the idea of slavery terrible (people were questioning the Bible's morality even back then), the pro-slavery side can be summarized in this simple statement from the Reverend Richard Fuller in 1845: "What God sanctioned in the Old Testament, and permitted in the New, cannot be a sin."[56]

While we (once again) don't have time or space to go into it, people who are interested in other ways the Bible has been used for terrible things are also encouraged to look into the Crusades, witch hunts, and the Christian influences on Hitler and the Holocaust. And keep in mind that big-time haters like the Ku Klux Klan also consider themselves true Christians.

What does all this show? It shows atheists are no more immoral than anybody else. Christians are not the original good people. In fact, you could even say that the Bible actually encourages some people into doing terrible things. Atheists know that things like slavery and murder are wrong without having some book or some priest have to tell them one way or the other.

If the only reason that you are "good" is because you think you're being watched by some big Guy In The Sky, then you have problems. If you are holding yourself back from committing murder just because you are afraid of hell, then I don't want to be around you. Brown-nosing God to get into heaven is not an attractive quality.

As one of my Christian students once admitted to me, "If I'm in trouble, and either a Christian can help me or an atheist, I honestly think I would want the atheist to help me. The Christian would probably help me because he knew he was supposed to, but the atheist would help me because he really wanted to."

I couldn't put it better myself.

Myth #2: Atheists Hate God

Another question many atheists get is, "Why are you so against God? Something must have happened to you to make you hate Him." This is pretty funny. It shows just how hard it is for them to imagine that God doesn't exist. Surely, I must believe in God, I just am mad at him or something.

The short answer to this question is, "I can't hate something that doesn't exist." I don't hate Santa Claus, or vampires or zombies. If the reason I say I don't believe in God is simply because I'm mad at him, then the reason you say you don't believe in the Easter Bunny is because you're mad at him. It's just a silly idea.

For the record, I did not set out to become an atheist. I was never abused by a priest or anything like that. Actually, I used to be a committed Christian. I went to a Catholic school, and went to church several times a week. I just happened to have a lot of questions about how Christianity and God worked. As I got older, my curiosity led me to explore the issues from many different angles; I used science, philosophy, and theology in my search for answers. I talked to priests. I studied the Bible, and the history of religion. I meditated.

I have always been a guy who wants to know the truth, even if it makes me uncomfortable. I would rather know a sad truth than believe a happy lie. And as I studied my questions about religion and God, a curious thing happened. It all fell apart easily…but it didn't go back together again. Without meaning to, I found myself unable to keep believing what I grew up believing. Just like I can't force myself to believe in Santa Claus anymore, I also couldn't force myself to believe in God anymore.

Despite reading the best arguments for God and Christ (like the proofs of God I presented earlier), they just didn't work if you looked at them logically. I realized that the only real way to be a full believer is to have a very strong blind faith. To believe it no matter what the evidence tells you. And I don't do blind faith.

So, as time went on, God just sort of dissolved back into the realm of fairy tales. There was no hate or anger involved, except, perhaps, for people I found out were lying to me about religious issues. There was a little bit of sadness at first, like letting go of a cherished idea always hurts. But letting go was a slow and natural process. Without an active effort to force God into my life, when I just let reality show itself to me, my faith melted away like snow at the beginning of spring.

Myth #3: Atheists Don't Believe in Anything

This is one of those myths that actually say more about the person that believes it than the atheists themselves. This myth is saying that if you don't believe in God, then there's nothing else to believe in. Without God, everything else, including your life, is a big zero.

If you think about it, all religious people, including Christians, are atheists about all gods of other religions. Christians don't believe in any gods except their one God from biblical tradition. As the saying goes, atheists just believe in one less god than Christians do.

It's also important to realize that not believing in God is not the same thing as not believing in an afterlife. They are different questions. I have friends that don't believe in God, but do believe in reincarnation. Others believe that death is just a transition into a different dimension of the universe, which is cut off from us while we are alive. God has nothing to do with their beliefs of what happens after death.

There is a huge difference between not believing in some *thing* and having no beliefs at all. It's not really possible to have *absolutely nothing* to believe in. If you are alive, you believe in things. Atheists believe all kinds of different things, and we don't all believe the same things. Atheists, just like everybody else, argue all the time about the meanings of different things.

The next question atheists get asked then, is "Well, what do you believe?"

Now what kind of question is that? Here, in a nutshell, is how the conversation usually goes:

> **Christian**: So if you don't believe in God, what do you believe?
>
> **Me**: Well, what do you believe?
>
> **Christian**: I believe in One God that created the universe and that he had a son named Jesus who saved all of us, even you, from eternal damnation.
>
> **Me**: And what else do you believe in?
>
> **Christian**: Huh? I just told you.
>
> **Me**: So that's all you believe in?
>
> **Christian**: No, of course not. I'm not sure what exactly you're asking.
>
> **Me**: And I don't know what you're asking. I don't believe in your God statement, but I believe in all kinds of things. I'm not exactly sure which beliefs you want to know. Do you want to know what I believe about the creation of the universe? Because I've been reading up on cosmology, so we could have a good discussion. Do you want to know if I believe in evolution? Yes, of course. It's as real as gravity. Do you want to know if I believe there should be more *Star Wars* movies? I would say yes, as long as George Lucas doesn't direct them. What else do you want to know?

Do you get the point? It's silly to ask anybody, not just an atheist, such a general question as "what do you believe?" You have to specify the subject of belief under discussion. But apparently, if you can't give a one sentence summary of the supernatural answer to everything, Christians get confused.

But that's the Christian's problem, not the atheist's.

Myth #4: Atheists Live a Sad and Empty Life

Well, the title of this book says what I think of this one.

A lot of people believe, however, that a person that doesn't believe in God must be really depressed. After all, she doesn't have the comfort of knowing that she is loved by a supreme being. She doesn't have hope of going to an eternally happy place after death. All she is stuck with is living with the knowledge that she is ultimately alone in a universe that doesn't care about her at all, without any meaning or purpose to existence. She may as well kill herself and put herself out of her misery if she really thinks there is no God to prevent it.

There is a point to this myth, however. If you start out as a Christian, it does take a lot of courage at the beginning to face up to reality as an atheist. I was a little scared and confused when I first realized that I didn't believe in God anymore. After all, it was not my intention to stop believing. But then I realized that being uncomfortable with the idea of no God didn't change anything. So I began to redefine my life.

Moving from Christian to atheist does require a lot of courage and work. I think many people are Christians just because they are afraid not to be. They just ignore the Big Questions of life, reassuring themselves that even though they don't understand a lot of things, God will take care of it all. The meaning of life is set out for them—worship God on earth so you can get to Heaven and happily worship him there forever.

However, as an atheist, life became a big adventure for me. I'm OK with not having set answers to the Big Questions. I like the search for them. More than that, I am not depressed or miserable. Honestly, I'm much happier now than I ever was as a Christian.

Christianity relies a lot on fear of punishment, and guilt over your thoughts and actions, to keep you in line. I never really felt that good about myself because I kept hearing about how terrible we all are without Jesus to save us. Becoming an atheist let me feel good about myself and my actions. I began to see the beauty in the world. Life became much more interesting when the "answers" weren't all just force-fed into me. I began to make my own sense of the world, sense that fit the world much more naturally than shoving myself awkwardly into a false box of religion.

So what about the meaning of life? Without religion to tell me the answer, why am I here? What am I supposed to do with my life?

For me, I realized that I'm not supposed to *discover* the meaning of life; it is not something you uncover like a detective. No, the meaning of life is something you *create*, like an artist. My life can have different meanings at different times in my life. It's OK to change it, to change myself.

That leads to the biggest effect atheism has brought to my life: Freedom. Leaving God behind, I began to feel freedom. Freedom like I had never felt before. As the existentialist philosophers point out, we are all free in this world, whether we want to be or not. Yes, it's a little scary at times. But everybody gets scared, no matter what you believe.

Atheism means you are free to demand evidence for other people's beliefs. You are free to communicate with others instead of with fairy tales. You are free to enjoy life without hurting other people. You are free to feel good about yourself. You are free to work out your own answers in the world. Don't get me wrong, it's hard work. You have a lot of responsibility, too. There's nothing certain.

I guess being an atheist is kind of like going mountain climbing. It takes practice to figure out how and where to step next. But the next step is totally up to you. It's hard work, but it's satisfying and powerful. And even if you never reach the very top, on each step of the way the view is awesome.

Part Five

Life Without God:
Words of Young Atheists

This is the part of the book where I stop talking. As the final section, I wanted to give an opportunity for other young adults to provide their perspectives on living life without God. I put the offer out on my blog for anyone high school or college age, who considered themselves to be atheist or agnostic, to contribute an essay for this book. I gave them no guidelines other than to write down what they would like other young people to understand about living as an atheist/agnostic.

These are their responses. They are of various ages, various backgrounds, various parts of the country. Some of the authors provide personal details such as contact information, some do not. Some of the essays read like journal entries. At least one of these essays was turned in as a high school report.

These are their own opinions, formed from their own lives. You may agree with them, you may not. They think and speak bravely, coming to grips with not believing in things that the majority of those around them do believe in, and for which they are sometimes treated with mistrust and disrespect.

Godless

Nicolas Soria
Grand Ledge, MI
Master.stghm@gmail.com
[This is an essay I wrote for a writing class in February 2006 explaining how and why I am Atheist.]

I do not believe in a god. Almost everyone I know claims to believe in God as a Christian. I never have liked God or wanted to believe in him. I have an issue where once someone brings up God or Jesus I see them as a slightly different person; it is rude to bring up religion in a real life conversation or in public. I do try to be tolerant and understanding of people's choices as long as they do not hurt others or spread hate. Yet, I still feel as though I am disliked for not believing in God.

Even as a child, I did not embrace the idea of a god controlling my life. Some of my friends said I would not go to Heaven if I said things such as, "God is stupid." I became a little afraid of not going to Heaven so I refrained from using anti-God statements. This probably was because my parents; although they advise religion, they had never preached to me and had seldom taken me to Church. In kindergarten and into 3rd grade I went to a Catholic school so I became tolerant of it, but that was the only pressure I felt to be religious.

The school I went to was St. Charles Boremeo. St. Charles was obviously a Catholic school operated by a parish, so we had to be involved with the Church. I would do all of the Church activities and events, but my involvement was not a spiritual thing the way it is for some people. As I said before, my parents were not the kind of parents who cared too much about anything religious; although we would occasionally go to Sunday mass. This idea of church as just something we did to be involved with the community has stuck with me as the best reason to go, followed by delicious communion wafers.

When I moved to Grand Ledge with my family, we stopped going to church and I attended public school. I stopped caring about God and religion, and it was not a part of my life aside from a few times when I was really upset with the computer and when I felt left out by friends who did attend Church and CCD (I still don't know what that stands for). At this stage in my life, around ten and eleven, I only believed that God might be there, but I didn't really think it had an impact on my life. This continued on through middle school. I would make jokes about God by mixing the Supreme Being with a casual situation such as, "What if the world was like a computer game, and things messed up because God went and got something to drink; then he came back and looked at the screen and said 'Oh crap!'" As dumb as the jokes were, I was still skeptical about God and never felt anything spiritual toward him.

My freshman year of high school was exciting. I was meeting new people, making new friends, and experiencing new things. It was not until high school that I realized there were a lot of religious people who I had never met because they were home schooled. I was listening to a radio show one night, and the host was talking about evolution and creation and how some people wanted creation taught in schools. When the radio host began taking callers they were talking about how the world was only 6000 years old and such. I did not know that there were people this crazy. I was disappointed by these people because I had just assumed everybody accepted evolution as the real life version and creation as the Bible story. I thought people lived with a line between real life and their religion; I was very wrong. Not only were there creationists calling in to the radio show, but there were also people in my school who believed these stories. One day, in my physical science class freshman year, someone who I had thought of as a pretty intelligent person started trying to use laws we learned in science to disprove the Big Bang and evolution. I couldn't understand how someone who was otherwise a respectable and mature person could believe in fairy tales.

I started realizing how many crazy people there are in the world, in this country especially, and in Grand Ledge. I was so used to people not talking about religion, but the new people I was meeting seemed to try to fully integrate religion and their life. I was not very fond or understanding of these ideas because I was not used to people thinking this way, and I found it to be silly. For about a month in my freshman year I criticized people about the way they worshiped God and Jesus on Xanga.com; it was so corny the way they worshipped. The criticizing I did was mostly just because they put God and Jesus as a hobby or interest on their member profile, I had always thought that religion was above being an "interest" for people. They thought of Jesus as a friend and not just a person to admire. Some of the people thought I was an atheist and started getting upset about it.

I did support Catholicism and Islam as religions to follow because they were similar, familiar, and supported God, but also had strict rules and traditions that Protestant Christians lacked. In my Xanga.com entries, I compared Muslims with people who believed they were "hardcore for Christ" and listened to Christian hard rock: Christians just listen to music and sing about God whereas Muslims make a big pilgrimage to their Holy City to worship God, as well as pray 5 times a day and fast. I also supported Catholicism because it had traditions and customs and could adjust to the times (even thought they do this slowly). Catholics have the sacraments, rosaries, incense, candles, and all sorts of interesting and elaborate traditions where these Protestant Christians were so boring and plain. Those were some of my favorite Xanga entries, and I started to think of religion as something to do for fun, and what is more fun than lighting candles and getting to eat bread and sip wine?

Today I consider myself Atheist and I am proud of it. Sometimes, I feel criminalized because I choose not to believe in lies. I don't have any soft spots for any particular faith anymore because they are all working to reverse the progress of humanity. Yet, as much as I find this ridiculous, I do not hate people for it. I just feel sorry for them and sometimes laugh (a search for "An Atheist's Nightmare" on YouTube is my favorite) I still celebrate Christmas and Easter and Lent for fun though, but it is just for fun. I don't have faith in a God.

Along with God comes an afterlife, and I do not believe in that either. Denying the existence of God is supposed to be the unforgivable sin, and I am damned to hell forever. There is nothing to worry about for me though, because there is no hell, nor a heaven. Someone said that we developed a belief in an afterlife to cope with the knowledge that we die, but if we continue to live after death then I will remember my past and regret things that I failed to accomplish or could have done better. I find the idea of ceasing to exist after death more of a relief because I will not have to worry about anything ever again.

I have never accepted God, and now that I know he does not exist, I do not have to worry about it. Even though the vast majority of people in my community do believe in this hokey stuff, I choose not to because it has no negative effect on my life and blind faith is not a virtue. I do not need a god or religion to have morals. It is more practical to find the right thing to do by using logic and thought, which is something the average "Christian" does anyway. I generally believe that as long as the behavior does not hurt individuals physically, or financially, it is acceptable.

The world would probably be a better place if all the energy put into religion were redirected to more productive activities.

Religion? Why?

Nicholas Burton, age 16
Canada
Nicholas.Burton.1@gmail.com

I like to think of myself as a fairly open person, as, no doubt, so do most people. That isn't to say, however, that I will accept anything or try anything, but that I will gladly listen to your argument or points of view. I don't suppose that it makes much sense to say that in order to be an open person, religiously, you have to accept everybody else's viewpoint, because that would be impossible. The best I, or anyone, can claim to do, is be willing to gladly argue, or discuss these topics. However, it can be confusing to try and arrange one's arguments while in the middle of said discussion.

So, I want to try and explain most of the points that confuse or annoy me in one concise location. That is not to say that this is, by any means, an end-point. The point of this is to bring up arguments which can then be further elaborated upon in open conversation.

Let's take, for a second, the view that the Christian God (ontologically, it would be more correct to label it as the Judeo-Christian God, but it is simpler, for the purpose of this piece of writing, to limit ourselves to a shorter name) created Earth, the Universe, people, and the whole shebang. My first question might be, "Why?" Why in God's name would God create us in his name? When I simply ask why, I tend to get the answer, "Because he loves us." When I explain that this is not an answer, because you cannot love something that cannot exist yet, most people are confused. Eventually, some say that "God created us as companions." That "he was lonely." Well, this is fine, I suppose. The question that next arises, then, is why God would create us as so far beneath him. If he wanted companions, he would have created friends, not things who worship him; this would seem to make it that we are not companions, so much as servants. An all-powerful, omnipotent god would be able to create something more compatible for friendship than us. Creating humans for companionship reminds me of the sixteen year old girl who gets herself pregnant because then, she figures, at least her baby will love her.

So my first question is, in summary, "Why?"

So, taking into account all that above, we realize that God might not have created us for companionship, but let's pretend, for a second, that he did. If he had, why would he have put all of the rules in the Bible into place? Why would the Ten Commandments, and all the rest be there to tell us what to do, and force us to pray, and conform, if all he wanted was a friend? Well, as far as I can see, this must be because 'life' as we know it, is simply a sorting process. If you live, and then, depending on how well you act, you might be able to go live with God, then the reason for living is to see who is worthy of heaven, right? Well, if religious people are to be believed, many, many things cause sin. So, many, many people must be going to hell, instead of heaven, right? (Anybody not Christian, or any sinning Christian). So then, my question here is *why would an omnipotent god have such a large margin of error?* If he is trying to create companions, why would he have so many of his creations not be good enough for him? (Less than half of the population of the earth is Christian, so he has less than 50% success rates). If he was omnipotent, he should have created every human as worthy, rather than much less than half. In fact, he should have no reason to create "life," or a screening process at all, if he was truly omnipotent. And this leads us to our next problem.

Now, follow me for a second, without a question here, will you? I see true omnipotence as impossible, because it is paradoxical. Firstly, of course, there cannot be more than one omnipotent being, because their powers would counter, and paradox would result. There is, of course, the problem of "Can God create a boulder too heavy for him to lift?" Most people answer, most idiotically, that, "Yes he could, but he won't." The problem with this, then, is it shows he is not omnipotent. If he could, then he would have created something he could not lift, and thereby become not omnipotent. On the other hand, if he could, but doesn't because he knows it will cause paradox and end his omnipotency, then he has still ended it, by creating something he cannot do, or will not do, because it will cause his own downfall, something that should be impossible for an omnipotent being.

Thus, we have uncovered our first fallacy in Christianity. It is impossible for "God," or any being, to be omnipotent.

So if we then decide that God is not omnipotent, as described in the Bible, what is he? Simply a more powerful being? Why is it worth worshipping, simply because he is more powerful than us? Aside from his lack of power, there are other reasons for not worshipping God. But, first, we must ascertain the level of power the devil has. It is said that God, being omnipotent, allowed the devil to revolt and leave hell with a considerable number of angels. Supposedly, God could have flicked his fingers and vanish the troublesome Lucifer, but he did not. He allowed the Archangel Michael (who was not supposed to be nearly as powerful as Satan, who, as an angel, was second only to God in his power, good looks, and intelligence. Thus, he fell because he refused to bend his neck to humans, and treat them as superior, as god wanted). So, God could have stopped a heavenly war, but he did not because he wanted to give his new favorite angel a chance to experience it. So we have a God who likes to let war happen, because he wants to see if people can handle it.

We also have a god who likes to get his hands dirty, and do some killing personally. Take, for instance, the old story of the Jews escaping from Egypt, the same god as that of the Christians. If he was displeased about the Egyptians keeping the Jews as slaves, then why would he not simply appear, and tell the Egyptians to release them? Or, why not simply vanish away the Jews and make them reappear in a better place? What possible justification could there be for a loving and benevolent god to murder every first born Egyptian, the huge majority of whom must be innocent? *So why would a god who not only enjoys watching fights, but enjoys personally slaughtering be worth worshiping, for any other reason than out of fear?* This leads us to our next problem.

Remember when we said we might not have been created as companions? Certainly, if God wanted companions, he would not want us to be afraid of him. And yet, if you are religious, you are a "God-fearing" person. God is perfectly willing to not force you to do something by simply making you do it, but he is willing to punish you if you don't do what he wants. Thus, I have to wonder: *If God did not create us to serve as companions, then did he make us as some sort of sick entertainment?* Are we here solely to entertain this "god"? Does he put burning hoops for us to jump through, merely to see if we get burnt? Remember the story of Job? God bargains with the devil over a believer. This person is the perfect Christian, so God and the devil have a bet to see whether the two immortals can crack and break the spirit of this poor man. Surely this is nothing but sick entertainment? We now have a god who not only enjoys watching war, and killing, but as also likes to gamble with the lives of those "companions" he loves?

This brings us to our next question. How powerful is Satan? Is he as powerful as God? The Christian answer must be no, and so too must be ours, because it is impossible to have two omnipotent beings (on the other hand, we showed that God cannot be omnipotent himself, so we can, perhaps, say they are both merely very powerful). Christians say that God was much more powerful than the Devil. So, why would he allow the devil to continue his actions? Well, to allow us freedom of will, they say. God wants us to have the opportunity to screw up, so he allows a person to tempt us to do so, while he remains relatively quiet. My question again has to do with the sorting process of God mentioned above. Not only should God not have to worry about us falling into evil (which we would not do, if created properly), it seems odd that he would risk it. If we are here as companions, which we are not sure of, then why would God allow the devil to misdirect those who might, otherwise, end up as good? As surely they would, in the absence of evil. It seems somewhat harsh to allow us to make our own mistakes, and then, once we do, leave us to rot in hell forever. If we are the children of God, as they always say, He should be more willing to interact to lead us along. Do you let your child wander in traffic, because you want to allow them free will? No, because their wrong decision will most likely result in their death. So why would God allow us to decide to follow him or not, when not following would result in us spending eternity suffering pain in the fires of hell? Perhaps not because he cares about us, but because he simply wants entertainment.

Any position can be picked apart eventually, given enough time. However, I believe that it is important that logic be applied to the belief in God. Whether or not one believes in God or follows a religion, I think that fundamentally, at least a basic amount of logic should be applied to something so important as a question that affects so many of us to some degree. Logic is like a skin draped over us, that we like to pretend goes all the way down. It's when we ignore logic, and use emotion and instinct, that we get acts which are more simplistic, and animalistic. When you decide things without logic, they tend to be either very simplistic and obvious, or nonsensical. Religion, like everything else, needs to be able to be willing to put itself under at least some level of some logical scrutiny. Otherwise, it risks being classified as simplistic at best, and nonsensical at worst.

Method, Meaning & Morality

Brandon Herr, age 21
Centreville, Virginia
BrandonHCville@aol.com

I am an atheist.

I am also a 21-year-old Caucasian male student that lives in the United States—a country where approximately 92% of its people claim to be theists (believe in the existence of one or more gods), and 80% of its people classify themselves as Christian.

Needless to say, many individuals wonder why I lack belief in a god and how I can be moral without that belief. Some argue that I do not believe simply because I do not want to believe. My lacking belief in theism has nothing to do with desire. I would happily believe in a promised, blissful eternity, just as I would happily believe there was a refrigerator-sized diamond in my backyard, but desire does not make either true. We must have reason to believe something is true. I have engaged in numerous discussions with theists and spent countless hours reading and researching various forms of evidence and arguments, and I still have yet to find a reliable and consistent reason to believe.

In my discussions with theists, many seem to use subjective and unanalyzed feelings to justify belief. They feel something, be it happiness, clarity, or some other sensation, when reading sacred texts, discussing religious topics, or performing religious ceremonies, and they seem to think that those feelings justify belief. Theists from every belief system—Catholics, Protestants, Jehovah's Witnesses, Mormons, Muslims, Buddhists, Hindus, etc.—make this claim. Not surprisingly, these belief systems contradict each other and, therefore, cannot all be true.

What the theists are feeling is not a gift from a god. They are simply experiencing an emotional response from adhering to personal values. For example, a computer programmer may get excited about reading, discussing, and coding a new program. An actor may get excited about reading, discussing, and acting in a new movie. Does that excitement mean there is some supernatural truth to programming or acting? Not in the least. The computer programmer may value being a good programmer, but may not value being a good actor. The actor may value being a good actor, but may not value being a good programmer. The programmer may experience pleasurable emotions from programming, but not from acting, and the actor may experience pleasurable emotions from acting, but not from programming.

This is why a theist experiences pleasurable emotions from being a good theist. There is nothing supernatural about it, and it certainly is not something that justifies belief.

These types of inconsistent and unreliable reasons for belief appear to stem partly from a widespread misunderstanding of words and partly from of a widespread misunderstanding of epistemology. Words allow us to communicate and epistemology answers the question, "How do we know if something is true?" When these misunderstandings filter into a discussion we can have trouble determining what is and is not true.

We use words so frequently that many of us take their meaning for granted. We even go so far as to assume that everyone defines and understands words the same way. In actuality, we often have different definitions and understandings of the same words, which easily creates confusion. The only way we can clear any confusion from our discussions is if we understand what words actually are.

Words are references to sensations. We use them to communicate, but this works only if we have a mutual understanding of what our words reference. When I say the word *cat*, I am communicating the particular sensations of a cat. A cat has a particular shape, size, mass, color, texture, motion, etc.

If someone were to ask, "What is the difference between a cat and a bear?" we immediately analyze the different sensations between a cat and a bear (for example: a bear is bigger than a cat). After we understand what sensations words reference, we can more effectively communicate those sensations.

For instance, I had a discussion with a theist where I was arguing that faith is not a reliable form of knowledge. The theist quickly retorted, "You have faith that the sun will rise tomorrow." The theist and I were referencing different sensations when we used the word "faith." In order to clear the confusion and make my point, I had to identify what different sensations were being referenced.

One of the sensations that I reference when I use the word "faith" is that faith is belief *without* evidence. Believing that the sun will rise tomorrow is belief *with* evidence. With that difference identified, the theist who argued that I "have faith the sun will rise tomorrow" must either accept that we are using different references of word "faith" and that "faith" in the theist's religion is *without* evidence, or the theist must contend that we are still referencing the same sensations and then supply evidence.

When I ask a theist for reasons to believe in god, I am asking for reliable proof that will let me know their god exists. When they use their feelings to justify believing in god, they are misunderstanding epistemology. Feelings are subjective, unreliable, and inconsistent, which makes them a poor source of knowledge.

Unfortunately, no knowledge is certain (Descartes' *"cogito ergo sum"* aside).* Instead, we must settle for degrees of confidence. Our degree of confidence in the truth of a proposition (a claim that something is true) depends on what method we use to analyze that proposition. Some methods produce more frequent and consistent results and are, therefore, more reliable forms of proof.

The most reliable method of proof is reason, which uses mathematical and logical proofs. Reason references concepts that can be quickly and easily tested by the mind and produces the broadest, most complete, and most consistent results. The propositions are simple and precisely defined.

For example we can say "Given A=B and B=C, then A=C" and be pretty confident the proposition "A=C" is true. This is undeniably clear from a mathematical standpoint. However, I can use the same proofs with the concept "cat." I can say, "If a cat (A) is a feline (B) and a feline (B) is an omnivore (C), then a cat (A) is an omnivore (C)." If A=B (cat = feline) and B=C (feline = omnivore), then A=C (cat = omnivore). We can repeatedly test this in our mind with any concept and have incredibly consistent results.

Reason demolishes the premise "God is omnipotent and benevolent." If God is omnipotent (A), then He can do whatever He wants. If God is benevolent (B), then He does not want humans to suffer. If God were both omnipotent (A) and benevolent (B), then He would create a universe where suffering does not exist (C). This can be viewed as "A+B=C." Since we live in a universe where suffering exists, it follows that God is either not A (not omnipotent), or God is not B (not benevolent), or suffering does not exist (not C).

The second most reliable method of proof is science. Science is a systematic method of observation and experimentation. These observations and experiments are repeated and recorded. The more those experiments confirm a proposition, the more confident we can be that the proposition is true. This process is typically less refined than reason and often requires a laboratory outside of the mind.

Theism is unscientific, because the proposition "theism is true" does not have supporting evidence. Many theists seem to think that if science cannot explain something then "God did it," but what reason do we have to believe it was the god Yahweh and not the god Krishna, or the god Flying Spaghetti Monster? Absolutely none. The theist has not supplied reliable evidence, and lacking that, we have no reason to believe.

The third most reliable method of proof is personal experience. This method is more reliable if we objectively and thoroughly analyze our experiences. Unfortunately, there are times when we cannot gather enough information or when we have not thoroughly processed our experiences, and we end up making poor decisions or believing untrue things.

Misjudgments are fairly common and have led to a number of supernatural conspiracies. Many used to believe that eclipses were caused by spells from witches and that lightning came from wrathful gods. History clearly shows us that once a supernatural claim is investigated, from eclipses to lightning and from leprosy to hallucinations, it turns out to be nothing more than misunderstood natural processes.

For example, one time I was walking down my hallway and out of the corner of my eye I caught some sort of quick-moving, bright light. I thought I saw a ghost. As I turned, the image vanished. I stood there for a moment in shock and disbelief. Then another car turned the corner and its headlights beamed through my window. The light hit the hallway at the same spot and moved at the same speed as my "ghost." When I first saw the light, I made an error in judgment. After I had gathered enough information, I knew that what I saw was not a ghost.

There are several other methods of proof. If you want a more detailed account of the reliability of the methods I have mentioned, I suggest reading *Sense and Goodness without God: A Defense of Metaphysical Naturalism* by Richard Carrier.

Once we have covered the basics of words and can effectively communicate, and once we are able to use this communication to understand epistemology and why it is reasonable to lack belief in a god, then we can see how it ties to morality.

As an atheist, I am frequently asked two questions, "How does an atheist define morality?" and "What reason does an atheist have to be moral?"

The definition of morality is ultimately a question of suffering and happiness. Anytime someone intentionally does something that makes anyone else needlessly suffer, we consider that action to be immoral.

This question becomes more complex when suffering is necessary for, or is outweighed by, happiness. For example, we may go through a painful surgery simply because not going through the surgery would cause greater suffering. We make these kinds of decisions all the time and they are personal decisions. Ultimately, we try to reduce our suffering and promote our happiness, which is why we adopt and follow a moral code.

I am always humored when theists ask me "Why be moral?" because they seem to take the question for granted. When I ask a theist, "Why be moral?" most respond: "God says do this, so I do it," but since they have failed to prove their god exists, this statement is irrelevant. Ultimately, atheists and theists are moral for the same reason: happiness.

When we act immorally or against our own values (honesty, reliability, compassion, etc), we experience suffering. We will be unable to experience the happiness from following our own morals and values if we deny the suffering we experience when we break them. Understanding words, epistemology, and morality is essential to effective communication, understanding what is true, and using that understanding to promote personal happiness. Without that understanding, life is a crapshoot. Life is much too short for that.

*René Descartes *cogito ergo sum* is commonly known as, "I think, therefore I am." This is the only knowledge that is absolutely certain. In order for us to experience something (such as a thought), we must exist.

Atheists in the Closet

Anatoly Venovcev, age 20
Waterloo, Ontario, Canada
tolyv@hotmail.com

Rule #1: Don't discuss religion unless it's with someone who shares your views.

Rule #2: Don't discuss politics unless it's with someone who shares your views.

Rule #3: If pulled into a discussion over religion or politics with a person you know has a different point of view, refrain from attacking, questioning, refuting, or disproving his points.

Those were once my three grand rules for communicating with people for three of my teenage years. They were concrete and unchangeable, created by me for a purpose that, I believed, will help me be a better communicator when talking to others. As a form of self-censorship, for a long time I thought they were a good idea.

Growing up in Texas, or in fact any community whose general views you do not accept, is an interesting experience. In many cases it's a very threatening and oppressive environment, though to be fair, Texas really isn't. However a touch of paranoia and a strict sense of what I believed was opposite to others gave me this stuffy feeling of oppression that I tried to compromise with in order to gain new friends and live peacefully in school without my views being questioned at every turn.

For one, my final years of high school were in a very conservative area. Though there surely were liberal people and leftist people who saw things from my perspective (you know, the general liberal package of pro-gay rights, pro-choice, pro-small business, pro-unions, pro-peace, and certainly procreation), they weren't the ones who ran the school either academically or popularly. The people I was around in the advanced placement classes were generally of the conservative stock who watched FOX news, went to church, and had their parents vote for the republican party. Around them I felt sort of an odd ball and claimed to be politically neutral (which partly I was) and dodge any teenage sludge-fest of twisted fact spewing in order to defend their party of choice. Personally I'd show support for the Green Party but that would have put me into the lunatic corner faster than saying that I was an atheist.

Yes, I am an atheist and that's where Rule #1, the most important rule, came to the list. Being an atheist with a clue, that is, being an atheist not just because it was a "rebellious" and "anti-establishment" thing to do (notice the quotations), was a very rare thing in my childhood. After a few small confrontations over religion, with people that went on to become my best friends, I was simply terrified of starting a religious conversation, much less in a religious environment where up to 80-90% of the class regularly attended church, sometimes more than once a week. I didn't want to be singled out, isolated, and persecuted for what I believed in. And even though I was already singled out for being a loner, a nerd, and a foreigner, I still didn't want to take an extra step and be natural over religion in fear of being cast even more into the depths of isolation and maybe even hostility.

I was probably overreacting; in fact now, when some of my friends know of my religious affiliations I do not get any cold shoulders. Generally, though, I am shunned from religious conversations that interest me greatly. Yet there was a fear, and there are still Christians, very strong Christians and good friends, who do not know where I stand. Probably if I did not delay and came out simply and said that I did not believe in any God I would have had a far more difficult road to fight before those people accepted me for who I am. So I remained quiet, I remained tolerant, and yes, when discussing religion I always defended my point and never questioned the other side's absurdities and attempts to convert me. I never offended, unless they thought my views were offensive, and I never brought up the conversation so that they would forget the incident. I justified it as "It's more peaceful that way."

This secrecy, much like my atheism, slowly grew and developed with my personality. My loss of faith, which did happen, was nothing dramatic of sorts. My family wasn't all too religious and we never went to church. I was baptized however into the Russian Orthodox faith and from what I remember the baptism wasn't all that bad. I cried, for some reason, but the old orthodox priest who baptized me was really patient and nice and the church, one of the old and fanciful ones, was very ornate and decorative. For that reason perhaps I never saw most religions beyond anything but harmless practices that periodically bring new degrees of art, music, and culture into the world.

My parents didn't care much for the church—my mother and her parents were a wishy-washy atheists while my father and his parents were wishy-washy Russian Orthodox—belief wasn't enforced and I was left to develop my religion freely. I lost my faith rather simply; I quit believing in a god because I quit believing in Santa Claus. A bit naïve, I know, and anti-climatic, but very effective and very reasonable considering there isn't sufficient evidence to believe in either (if you say that the former is proven by the presence of the gospels, give me a few weeks and I'll write you the Santa Claus Bible).

Moving to America at age ten things didn't change much or really weren't aggravated because children are bit apathetic toward religion in elementary school. Nobody cared what I believed in and nobody asked. I remained an atheist of course because, as usual, there wasn't any proof for any god. To the best memory can offer, real questions over religion began in sixth grade in a place that is somewhat famous for valuing its religion: Oklahoma.

It was here that I really came into understanding that what I believed was something different than what other people believed in. A person even tried to get me to go to church. I actually did go with my family; needless to say we didn't stay long. In a funny incident I was once asked if I attended church, I said no. The other boy replied that I should and when asked why he simply replied "I don't know, just because." This was in sixth grade mind you, but I'll let the readers draw their own conclusions, as it is not the topic of this essay.

In late middle school my ideas over religion started to bloom. I was part of an Internet forum by that time, a game forum but they discussed "intellectual" things there as well (as much as middle and high school can discuss "intellectual" things) and that's where many hot religious discussions happened. In course of a few conversations though I saw how futile it was convincing people that I am right and dropped it. I dropped discussing politics soon after for the same reasons of futility. In the end I realized the same thing that plagues all free-thinking debaters in the form of the insurmountable wall of faith that one must breach in order to get anywhere and hence I quit arguing.

The rules followed after a brief encounter over religion and yet another conversion attempt. I refused to discuss religion anymore. I followed those rules. Whenever somebody asked me if I went to church, I quickly changed the topic of the conversation (and it worked) and when ever I heard Christians fuming about "those people" who "refused to believe in God" when "all of the things in the Bible were proven true," I did not join in to defend my views. For three years I compromised, I mitigated, and I dodged any religious or political question shot in my direction and in the end, it started to hurt.

As any greatly opinionated person would understand, after years of quiet and even sitting through a long, drawn out conversation where my Christian friends discussed "the awesomeness of their God" without uttering a word, I began to get angry with myself. Here I was, a person no dumber than them, no more inferior, no more ignorant, hiding behind the mask of muteness. It was almost as if I did not have any views, any ideas, any theories of my own and relinquished all power to choose and think for good grades in school (as some people thought). It was demeaning, demeaning to both me and my ideas and sitting listening to religious zealots speak, after a while I just had enough.

It didn't come suddenly, it came in stages. I slowly began talking about religion, just mild thought fancies at first. Like a conversation with a relatively tolerant Christian friend of mine over the shortcomings of the Biblical text or a blog entry on how, if God was so powerful and omnipotent, why does He want a world bowing down and reminding Him of that fact? (If anyone is wondering, the answer to that question is "Don't humanize God, you godless infidel.") Then I picked up the pace, read a book on atheism (*Why I Am Not a Christian* by Bertrand Russell, I wouldn't recommend it) and earned enough footing again to stand on. I participated in another religious discussion, but really, they are still boring.

Finally, I got tired of feeling inferior and just spoke out. Or rather a Christian friend did for me when he asked me if I was an atheist. I said yes and we had a discussion where the only thing he proved was just how absurd some of the religious pretexts are and that was really the flowering of my openness. After three years, I'm actually not afraid of saying that I'm an atheist if anyone asks. And why should I? What is it about atheism that's wrong? Or inferior? Dangerous? Immoral? Shortsighted? Inhuman? There's nothing of that in atheism. I am as much a person as anyone with any different religion and to them, in the worst case scenario, I'm just a person with a different view than theirs. At best, I could be a way to another, more natural view of the world, but it's not in my character to convert. I don't care what anyone believes in, but if asked, I will speak my mind and ask only for simple acceptance.

This atheist is out of the closet.

And really, why shouldn't I be? An atheist is not a synonym for "monster" or "murderer." An atheist is just a synonym for just what it means: "A" meaning "without" and "theos" meaning "God." No gods, no miracles, no saints, no heroes; there are only men in this world, just like it should have been all along. It's not like I am worse for it. I am intelligent, friendly, and sometimes humorous. I graduated early and still was ranked fifth in my class. I like sunsets and stormy weather. I listen to The Beatles and I listen to Bach. I exercise, go fishing, ride my bike. I enjoy the company of my friends despite them being conservative Christians. I like the company of smart and attractive girls, though I never had a girlfriend. I don't hate or get angry easily. I never had a suicidal thought or seriously considered hurting someone. I never made a girl cry or hotly fought a friend (things that my Christian friends can't brag about). I don't drink, or smoke. The strongest drug I have ever taken was an aspirin five years ago. I support peace and aid to the poor of the world. I'll always advise a friend not to get an abortion and always to have a condom around (ironically yes, on a personal level I don't want people getting abortions). I will not rape, murder, hurt, cheat, or act irresponsibly. I also like flowers and tie-dye shirts and French love songs and the color pink and I'll tell anyone that liking those things won't make you gay.

And yet, there are people out there who at a blink of an eye will tell me that just because I am an atheist, just because I don't believe in their god, I am automatically less fulfilled, less satisfied, less loving, less kindly, less selfless, than them and those other people who believe in the same. It is that which is most confusing to me and it is that which is the most wrong. To all those who question, doubt, or disbelieve: I think it is time for the world to accept us for who we are as people and we should not hide in the shadows and let them distort us even further. With a heart, a mind, a spirit, and a will, how can anyone be somehow inferior? Life tells us and experience affirms that religion alone does not make a man much like race, nationality, sex, social status, political affiliation, affluence, or sexual preference have shown the same. Only a man can make the man. So while to anyone I may be an atheist, to myself, the world, and anyone who will listen, above all, I am also a human being.

To Hell with Justice

Aaron Farish
Kansas City, Kansas
aaron.farish@gmail.com

When Albert Einstein said, "God does not play dice," he was not supporting Christianity. In a way, he may have been disproving it. Einstein was simply inferring that nothing happens by chance, everything can be predicted. This idea of predictability supports a branch of philosophy called determinism, the idea that everything is determined. Unfortunately for some Christians, if determinism is correct, it would mean many essential concepts of Christianity such as free will, responsibility, and most importantly, the existence of a hell, are not true. Determinism offers significant evidence to refute not only these biblical concepts but also the idea of justice. In order to understand this claim, you must first know what determinism is.

Imagine you're playing a game of pool. In order to hit the ball in a pocket, you must predict where it will land by how you shoot it. If you take into account all of your circumstances and use that information accurately, your prediction will be correct, and you will make the shot. Einstein thought that everything could be predicted in the same way. Since every event is caused by an action, every event can be predicted by studying the action. By studying the shot accurately you know you will hit the ball in the pocket. Einstein's quote "God does not play dice" implies creation did not happen by chance.

Predictability and determinism go hand in hand. If you've ever wondered why something happened, you'd realize there's always a reason behind it. Determinism is the idea that everything happens because it must. If you were to toss a penny you would assume it would hit the ground, any other outcome would be impossible. In that case, the outcome of the penny hitting the ground was pre-determined, it had to happen. Every event acts in the same way. The penny had to hit the ground because it was effected by physical applications: gravity, power, resistance, friction. The penny would not just float in the air because the forces affecting it would not allow it to. All events are affected by those same forces of nature that affect the penny; therefore, those events are also pre-determined.

Determinism also suggests that these events would include human actions. And if human actions are determined, it would mean people hold no free will. Anything you've done has been determined and whatever you will do has been determined.

Have you ever done something bad, and been told by someone, "You didn't have to do that"? Determinism says that, yes, you did have to do that. In fact, you had to do everything you've ever done. Why? A simple deterministic belief that everything is inevitable, which means everything that happens, or happened, had to happen. Say you're playing catch with a friend. You throw the ball but your friend doesn't catch it. Initially you blame it on your friend's lack of skill for not catching the ball, but then you start to think, well, it's not really his fault if he's no good at catching, it's just wired in his genes or something. Then you start to think, maybe it is his fault for not practicing. This is where a lot of people tend to stop thinking and start blaming, but just as you assumed your friend was not responsible for his lack of skill, the same applies to his lack of obedience. There could be many reasons why he does not practice, even if he didn't want to, he had no way of controlling that. If he didn't want to practice, it is either because of the effect of DNA, past experience(s), or both, all of which he cannot control. The only thing that controls his actions are previous actions; by retracing events you could come to the conclusion that your friend had no control over a past action, or actions before his birth, that would eventually lead to his decision to not practice, therefore, having no control over the event, he is not responsible.

Remember the belief of predictability: everything that happens can be predicted if given enough information. By knowing the effect an event has on the universe, you can predict, or determine the outcome. Your friend had no control whether or not he catches the ball; it is all predetermined due to a chain of events that would end up creating the present situation. If you are sitting at home right now reading a book, that situation is inevitable, it had to happen, and there was no way it could not have.

If you do anything, there's a reason behind it, that reason also has a reason behind it, and the next. Because every action is effected by another action, every action is just an effect of an initial action taking place at the beginning of time in which you unquestionably had no control over. If you don't have control, you have no free will, and hold no responsibility.

Determinism is often frowned upon due to its lack of cooperation with other ideas and beliefs. Those beliefs include a very powerful one everyone knows as justice. Justice is an idea many don't understand, but it's actually pretty simple: punishment suitable for the crime. In American they do this by a sentencing. For example, if murder was pre-meditated, the charge would be life in prison, or in some cases death. This is considered just because since the murderer took the victim's life away, the same should be done to the murderer. But determinism says this is wrong! If no one is responsible for his or her actions, then of course it is not just or right to punish someone at all. You wouldn't kill someone who was forced to kill another person, but that is exactly what the modern justice system does. Remember, determinism says that no person is responsible for any action, bad or good. If this is true, any punishment at all would be unjust. Why then does justice prevail? Simple, the justice system does more than punish; it corrects the people by punishment, as well as set a moral example for its citizens. If you were to punish a child, say, send them to time out, it is because you are trying to correct them, teach them that there are consequences for their actions. Although determinism suggests that all punishment is wrong, it works for society to correct, teach, and set an example for the people of the society.

When you think of punishment you think of two things: prison, and hell. The Bible defines hell as being eternal punishment for sin committed during one's lifetime. If you commit a sin, without being forgiven by God of all your sin, you will go to hell. Pretty simple, follow the the Bible and you won't suffer eternal punishment. But determinism contradicts the Biblical claim of God being just, such as in Deuteronomy 32:4 ("He is the Rock, his work is perfect: for all his ways are judgment: a God of truth and without iniquity, just and right is he."—King James Version). Remember, any punishment at all is unjust, but it works to correct people the same way as putting a child in time-out. Although, if you were trying to correct a child you would not leave your them in time-out for eternity, otherwise the process of correcting them would be defeated. If God simply wanted to correct the punished he would not have them spend eternity in hell. Determinism presents the idea that people are without free will and responsibility. It would not be right to punish someone eternally for sins over which they had no control. God cannot be just if hell is real, and hell cannot be real if God is just.

If you were God, would you put a baby in hell for crying? Would you put a puppy in hell for wagging its tail? Of course you wouldn't! Yet according to the Bible God does all the time. The baby had to cry, the puppy had to have wagged its tail, just like you and everyone who has sinned, had to have sinned. It was determined.

Einstein was not trying to refute the Bible, or even mention religion in his statement. He was a physicist writing about his thoughts on quantum physics. His idea does not affect determinism, it only relates to it. Determinism is a profound and intriguing idea, and there's more to it than questioning justice and rejecting hell. Although some may decide to reject determinism, no one can deny that there's a reason behind everything, and this is perhaps the strongest evidence in support of determinism. By accepting determinism as a fundamental belief it could enable you to apply critical thought to every action and abandon the burden of society's imposed moral standards. By relying solely upon your reasoning ability, you could fulfill your potential as a member of a complex society.

Pascal's Wager

Tony Sommer, age 15
Independence, Kansas
atheistthoughts@hotmail.com

I have only been researching theology, specifically Christianity, for just over a year now. I have already learned much, not only about the Bible and arguments for God, but also about the average Joe's perception of the evidence. It is a very rare person indeed that holds a theological belief that they can back up, and Christianity's no exception. Most people who haven't investigated it must have two main arguments: Cosmological (the "first cause" argument) and Pascal's Wager. The Cosmological argument is easily disposed of if you know enough about laws of nature such as the first law of thermodynamics. However, I will not be going into the Cosmological argument. This essay will be about Pascal's Wager.

Blaise Pascal was a mathematician in the 17th century. His claim to fame for theologians, however, is his argument, not so much for the existence of God, but for the belief in God. Any open atheist has heard this at least once. It goes something like this: if you believe in God and you're right, then you go to heaven and lose nothing. If you believe in God and you're wrong than you lose nothing. But if you don't believe in God and you're right then you gain nothing. If you don't believe in God and you're wrong, then you lose everything. So it's much more reasonable to believe in God, right?

In fact, this argument has many flaws. One is that it assumes there are only two choices, Christianity or atheism. Many other religions believe in heaven and hell. So, according to Pascal's Wager, we should carefully weigh each religion, not on the basis of evidence, but on the basis of how bad each hell is and how good each heaven is. I don't know about you, but I wouldn't mind having my own private virgins in heaven, so my choice would be Islam. Christianity's heaven consists of being with God in heaven. No fountains of wine, no virgins, no puppy dogs or kitty cats. OK, so maybe their hell is really bad. I mean, fire, brimstone, torture, what could be worse? Well, you'll be disappointed if you think that's what the Bible says hell is. Most of what Christians know about hell is from the New Testament. Jesus is our only source of knowledge about hell. He says there'll be gnashing of teeth, but other than that doesn't get too in depth. It seems all hell is a separation from God. I think I can picture a worse hell than that.

There is an assumption in Pascal's Wager that a Christian loses nothing. This is referring to the afterlife, of course, but it still applies to our 'real' life. Let's crunch some numbers real quick. When I was catholic, I went to church once a week for one hour. Since there are about 52 weeks in a year, that's 52 hours a year. Let's say you have a minimum wage (a bit more than $5 an hour) job. If instead of going to church, you worked at that job, you would make over $260 a year. Since there about 160 million Christians in the United States, that would be $41.6 billion a year that could be made. Don't forget about the church income. When I went to church with my mom I know she gave about $50 every month or two. Since this covered our whole family, I'll assume that an average of $1 per follower is given to the church every week. That would be another $8.3 billion per year, which brings our total to $49.9 billion. There's also the incalculable amount of time wasted on mission trips, the immense damage done in our politics, and other wastes of time such as writing books. We also shouldn't forget the time wasted by people trying to work in spite of Christians. To say the Christian loses nothing might be true, the damage that it passes on to our society makes the wager suddenly seem a hell of a lot less reasonable.

Christians who convert for this reason lose something else, the knowledge that they believe the truth. The atheist who has investigated the claims is confident that they have the truth, but the Christian would be blindly hoping their belief is true. Imagine your most beloved family member died. Would you want to wait until you died to know what happened? Pascal's Wager is asking us to say we would rather not face the truth, no matter how awful it may be. Atheism requires a lot of courage to know that there is no big guy in the sky who will protect you and no heaven to go to after your death. Pascal's Wager asks us to be cowards, only believing because we are scared of finding out the truth.

Pascal's Wager proponents also seem to forget that all of today's religions might be wrong. Perhaps God doesn't like people worshipping him. God could easily send people who worship him to hell, and send atheists to heaven. This God is no more unreasonable than the Christian God who sends people to hell because they fail to follow all of God's ridiculously tough laws. This crazed God actually set it up so that humans would fail, so that he could come to the rescue in the form of Jesus. But this only works if you worship him. Is a God who is so cocky that he demands worship in the face of eternal punishment any more likely than a God who will send people to hell because he *doesn't* like worship? There are other possible Gods that will send people to hell for various "crimes," eating the wrong foods, worshipping without covering your head, or for working on certain days. God might not even care if you worship or not. He might send everybody to heaven. If anybody questions how reasonable these Gods are, you can always respond with the Christian's response to failed prayer, "God acts in mysterious ways."

All these objections are perfectly reasonable, but there is one main reason why Pascal's Wager fails. It's not proof; it's just a giant emotional appeal. Only those who wish to be ignorant in favor of comforting myths will fall for Pascal's Wager.

Conclusion

So we have reached the end of this exploration. Though we have barely scratched the surface of this huge (and hugely important) subject, hopefully you have learned a greater appreciation for the atheist position, no matter what your religious faith is. Also, hopefully you have been inspired to think more deeply about what you believe and even identified parts of this topic that you would like to learn more about on your own.

If you consider yourself an atheist or agnostic, perhaps you are ready to learn more, do more, meet others like you. Maybe you feel like "coming out of the closet" and proclaiming your religious independence with confidence and style.

If you consider yourself a Christian, hopefully you have a greater appreciation for why people leave religion behind. Hopefully you have a greater respect for your friends and relatives who tell you that they don't believe in any god, because it takes a lot of courage to do so. Perhaps most of all, I hope you will realize that you need to stop trying to convert atheists to Christianity. It is fine to live your faith openly, but you must allow atheists to live their non-faith openly. No matter how sure you are that you're right, trying to force it on other people doesn't do any good, and only makes you look like an intolerant bully. If you feel you must pray for atheists, you have that right. But then leave it alone, and let your god do the work.

We are in an age where communication and information flows more freely than it ever did before. So this book does not have to be the end of our conversation. In fact, you have the right to respond to me, because conversations work two ways.

I would love to hear from you about your reactions to this book. Perhaps you have an experience or perspective of your own that you would like to share with me. Perhaps you have your own opinions that you thought I left out of this little book. Whatever your thoughts, I'd like to hear them. I can't promise to contact you back, but I will try.

You can reach me in several different ways:

If you have something you would like to share with me directly, you can email me at happilygodless@gmail.com.

You are also welcome to join my ongoing blog about this topic on Xanga: (http://www.xanga.com/happily_godless). The readers of the blog have been of great help to me as I finished writing the book. It's also a great place to go to connect with other young atheists/agnostics and figure out next steps.

And, of course, you can find me on MySpace (look for the name "happilygodless") and Facebook (again, "happilygodless").

Thanks for reading, and remember to always think bravely!

Notes

1. Jennifer Michael Hecht, *Doubt: A History* (New York: HarperCollins, 2004), 4.

2. http://www.talkorigins.org/faqs/comdesc/section2.html#atavisms_ex2

3. http://www.pbs.org/wgbh/evolution/change/grand/

4. http://www.infidels.org/library/modern/richard_carrier/addendaB.html#Sagan

5. Michael Shermer, *How We Believe: Science, Skepticism, and the Search for God.* (New York: Henry Holt, 2000), 186.

6. http://www.religioustolerance.org/chr_jcno.htm

7. http://ancienthistory.about.com/od/holidaysfestivals/a/solsticeceleb_4.htm

8. Randel Helms, *Gospel Fictions* (New York: Prometheus Books, 1988), 24.

9. Earl Doherty, *The Jesus Puzzle* (Ontario: Age of Reason, 1999), 89.

10. Tim Callahan, *Secret Origins of the Bible* (Altadena, California: Millenium Press, 2002), 390.

11. John Shelby Spong, *Rescuing the Bible From Fundamentalism* (New York: HarperCollins, 1991) 80, 94.

12. Randel Helms, *Gospel Fictions* (New York: Prometheus Books, 1988), 35.

13. John Shelby Spong, *Rescuing the Bible From Fundamentalism* (New York: HarperCollins, 1991) 213-214.

14. Randel Helms, *Gospel Fictions* (New York: Prometheus Books, 1988), 48,50.

15. Wilhelm Schneemelcher, ed. *New Testament Apocrypha* (Louisville, Kentucky: Westminster/John Knox Press), 417.

16. Tim Callahan, *Secret Origins of the Bible* (Altadena, California: Millenium Press, 2002), 377.

17. For an interesting (and often heated) discussion of viewpoints about the chronology of Jesus, see http://en.wikipedia.org/wiki/Chronology_of_Jesus%27_birth_and_death

18. See note 17, above.

19. Wikipedia is the home to a fascinating debate of the importance of Mithras to Christianity: http://en.wikipedia.org/wiki/Mithraism

20. Tim Callahan, *Secret Origins of the Bible* (Altadena, California: Millenium Press, 2002), 381

21. Tim Callahan, *Secret Origins of the Bible* (Altadena, California: Millenium Press, 2002), 379-381.

22. Wilhelm Schneemelcher, ed. *New Testament Apocrypha* (Louisville, Kentucky: Westminster/John Knox Press, 1990), 461.

23. Wilhelm Schneemelcher, ed. *New Testament Apocrypha* (Louisville, Kentucky: Westminster/John Knox Press, 1990), 444-449, 462-465

24. Tim Callahan, *Secret Origins of the Bible* (Altadena, California: Millenium Press, 2002), 357, 359.

25. Tim Callahan, *Secret Origins of the Bible* (Altadena, California: Millenium Press, 2002), 360.

26. Tim Callahan, *Secret Origins of the Bible* (Altadena, California: Millenium Press, 2002), 367.

27. Lee Strobel, The Case for Christ (Grand Rapids, Michigan: Zondervan, 1998), 80.

28. Tim Callahan, *Secret Origins of the Bible* (Altadena, California: Millenium Press, 2002), 367.

29. Susan Jacoby, *Freethinkers: A History of American Secularism* (New York: Henry Holt, 2004), 19.

30. Susan Jacoby, *Freethinkers: A History of American Secularism* (New York: Henry Holt, 2004), 24.

31. Susan Jacoby, *Freethinkers: A History of American Secularism* (New York: Henry Holt, 2004), 24.

32. Susan Jacoby, *Freethinkers: A History of American Secularism* (New York: Henry Holt, 2004), 24.

33. David L. Holmes, *Faiths of the Founding Fathers* (New York: Oxford, 2006), 81.

34. Susan Jacoby, *Freethinkers: A History of American Secularism* (New York: Henry Holt, 2004), 42-43.

35. Jennifer Michael Hecht, *Doubt: A History* (New York: HarperCollins, 2004), 355.

36. Jon Meacham, American Gospel (New York: Random House, 2006), 8.

37. David L. Holmes, *Faiths of the Founding Fathers* (New York: Oxford, 2006), 39-48.

38. Susan Jacoby, *Freethinkers: A History of American Secularism* (New York: Henry Holt, 2004), 18.

39. Susan Jacoby, *Freethinkers: A History of American Secularism* (New York: Henry Holt, 2004), 18.

40. Susan Jacoby, *Freethinkers: A History of American Secularism* (New York: Henry Holt, 2004), 20.

41. Susan Jacoby, *Freethinkers: A History of American Secularism* (New York: Henry Holt, 2004), 21.

42. Susan Jacoby, *Freethinkers: A History of American Secularism* (New York: Henry Holt, 2004), 25-26.

43. Susan Jacoby, *Freethinkers: A History of American Secularism* (New York: Henry Holt, 2004), 27.

44. Susan Jacoby, *Freethinkers: A History of American Secularism* (New York: Henry Holt, 2004), 30.

45. Susan Jacoby, *Freethinkers: A History of American Secularism* (New York: Henry Holt, 2004), 31.

46. Susan Jacoby, *Freethinkers: A History of American Secularism* (New York: Henry Holt, 2004), 31.

47. Susan Jacoby, *Freethinkers: A History of American Secularism* (New York: Henry Holt, 2004), 32.

48. David L. Holmes, *Faiths of the Founding Fathers* (New York: Oxford, 2006), 70.

49. http://www.wallbuilders.com/resources/search/detail.php?ResourceID=5

50. http://www.yale.edu/lawweb/avalon/diplomacy/barbary/bar1796t.htm, for example.

51. One such place is http://www.tektonics.org/qt/tripoli.html

52. http://www.tektonics.org/qt/tripoli.html

53. Susan Jacoby, *Freethinkers: A History of American Secularism* (New York: Henry Holt, 2004), 287.

54. Sam Harris, *Letter to a Christian Nation* (New York: Knopf, 2006), 20.

55. Richard Dawkins, The God Delusion (New York: Houghton Mifflin, 2006), 254.

56. Sam Harris, *Letter to a Christian Nation* (New York: Knopf, 2006), 16.

LaVergne, TN USA
18 December 2009
167421LV00002B/5/A